THE
EVERYTHING®
LOGIC
PUZZLES BOOK
VOLUME 2

Dear Reader,

Welcome to my second collection of logic puzzles, designed like the previous volume (*The Everything® Logic Puzzles Book, Volume 1*) to provide you with hours and hours of fun, although you might at times become frustrated. I believe that you should not get discouraged, especially if you try, because I have attempted to make the book as user-friendly as I could without diluting the challenge of the puzzles.

As in the previous volume, I have taken nothing for granted. Even if you are an expert at puzzles, you might still enjoy the ones I have created here and perhaps how I have explained their solutions. I have planned each chapter around a particular puzzle theme and laid out the puzzles in each section of the chapter in order of difficulty. If you ever get stuck on a particular hard nut, just go to the answer section at the back. There you will find the solution completely explained.

My passion for puzzles started in childhood, when I would do all the puzzles at the back of comic books rather than read the comics themselves! My hope is that this book, like its predecessor, will impart to you the enthusiasm I have always felt in this area of human thinking.

Marcel Danesi, PhD

Welcome to the EVERYTHING® Series!

These handy, accessible books give you all you need to tackle a difficult project, gain a new hobby, comprehend a fascinating topic, prepare for an exam, or even brush up on something you learned back in school but have since forgotten.

You can choose to read an Everything® book from cover to cover or just pick out the information you want from our four useful boxes: e-questions, e-facts, e-alerts, e-ssentials. We give you everything you need to know on the subject, but throw in a lot of fun stuff along the way, too.

We now have more than 400 Everything® books in print, spanning such wide-ranging categories as weddings, pregnancy, cooking, music instruction, foreign language, crafts, pets, New Age, and so much more. When you're done reading them all, you can finally say you know Everything®!

PUBLISHER Karen Cooper

MANAGING EDITOR Lisa Laing

COPY CHIEF Casey Ebert

ASSISTANT PRODUCTION EDITOR Jo-Anne Duhamel

ACQUISITIONS EDITOR Zander Hatch

SENIOR DEVELOPMENT EDITOR Brett Palana-Shanahan

EVERYTHING® SERIES COVER DESIGNER Erin Alexander

THE
EVERYTHING®
LOGIC
PUZZLES
BOOK
VOLUME 2

200 more puzzles to increase
your brain power

Marcel Danesi, PhD

Adams Media
New York London Toronto Sydney New Delhi

I dedicate this book to my three grandchildren, Alex, Sarah, and Charlotte. They are the solution to the puzzle of my own life.

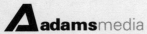

Adams Media
An Imprint of Simon & Schuster, Inc.
57 Littlefield Street
Avon, Massachusetts 02322

An Everything® Series Book.
Everything® and everything.com® are registered trademarks of Simon & Schuster, Inc.

First Adams Media trade paperback edition SEPTEMBER 2017

ADAMS MEDIA and colophon are trademarks of Simon and Schuster.

For information about special discounts for bulk purchases, please contact Simon & Schuster Special Sales at 1-866-506-1949 or business@simonandschuster.com.

The Simon & Schuster Speakers Bureau can bring authors to your live event. For more information or to book an event contact the Simon & Schuster Speakers Bureau at 1-866-248-3049 or visit our website at www.simonspeakers.com.

Interior design by Colleen Cunningham

Manufactured in the United States of America

10 9 8 7 6 5 4 3 2 1

ISBN 978-1-5072-0415-3

Contents

Acknowledgments

As with the previous volume, my sincere thanks go out to my wonderful agent, Grace Freedson, who made this possible in the first place, and my editor at Simon & Schuster, Zander Hatch, who has been absolutely delightful in getting me through the whole writing process. I also must thank my wonderful wife, Lucia, for putting up with all my grumpiness during the realization of this book.

Introduction

There are countless studies about the importance of keeping your brain active and engaged to help slow down the degenerative process of aging. And it's true that a mind that is challenged to find patterns and solve problems is more aware and involved. The problem is that most people don't get enough of this type of brain stimulation in their everyday lives. Enter logic puzzles. These play with pattern, meaning, arrangement, and organization in a fun way and ask you to deduce or conclude something from a given set of facts. They are an entertaining (and challenging) exercise for your brain.

At first you may think that challenging your brain sounds more like a chore than a fun activity, but you'd be surprised. With the puzzles in this book you will find hidden figures, decipher number patterns, plan out how to cross rivers, and more. You'll be using such logic skills as deduction, reasoning, and inference in an enjoyable and fun way.

This book contains 200 logic puzzles that will boost your ability to figure things out systematically. If you are new to such puzzles, don't worry; this book is designed to guide you through them and help you learn how to think logically. In each chapter, you will find "illustration puzzles" that go through the steps involved in solving a specific type of puzzle. At the back, you will find not only answers to the puzzles but full explanations of the reasoning used in solving them, so you will know *why* the answer is what it is. Additionally, each chapter has a range of puzzles from easy to moderate to difficult so that you can build up confidence gradually.

Using logic and a bit of imagination you'll have fun uncovering a pattern or a twist in a puzzle, ending up with the satisfying "Aha!" moment. This book will thus give you hours of fun that will improve your logic skills for solving both puzzles and many of the situations of everyday life. Enjoy!

CHAPTER 1

Figure-Counting Puzzles

Nothing exists until or unless it is observed.
—WILLIAM BURROUGHS (1914–1997)

Discerning figures, shapes, and patterns—to literally "figure things out"—is a critical skill in everyday life and has been a subject of interest throughout time. For example, the great ancient philosopher Plato believed that humans are born with "ideal forms" in the mind and then use them to detect shapes in the real world, and the branch of psychology known as Gestalt psychology studies how people come to perceive objects as forms and assign meaning to them. This chapter contains puzzles that will put your powers of perception and observation, guided by logical analysis, to the test. You will be required to count specific figures (squares, rectangles, triangles, circles, and so on) that might be embedded in larger figures. These puzzles are exercises in "whole-part" thinking.

How Many Figures?

Some people find the puzzles in this section to be among the most frustrating of all types, since it is not unusual to come up with different answers each time you count the same figures. Let's do a very simple one together.

▸ ILLUSTRATION ◂

This puzzle asks you to count how many complete four-sided figures (squares and rectangles) there are in the diagram altogether. A four-sided figure can be composed of smaller constituent figures, like pieces in a LEGO set or a jigsaw puzzle.

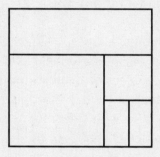

You have to be careful because the puzzle asks you to identify all the squares and rectangles within the diagram—including the large one that contains them all! Always keep in mind that there are "stand-alone figures" and "assembled figures." The best approach to these puzzles is to number all the segments you see. Let's start with the stand-alone figures.

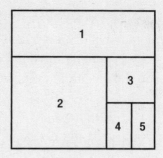

As you can see, figures 1, 2, 3, 4, 5 are squares or rectangles that stand alone. Let's mark these down as follows.

STAND-ALONE FIGURES

1. 1
2. 2
3. 3
4. 4
5. 5

Let's now count the squares and rectangles that are assembled:

ASSEMBLED FIGURES

6. $1 + 2 + 3 + 4 + 5$ (These pieces make up the large square with all the internal figures. It is the easiest one to miss!)
7. $2 + 3 + 4 + 5$
8. $3 + 4 + 5$
9. $4 + 5$

As you can see, there are nine four-sided figures in total—five stand-alones and four assembled figures. That's all there is to it.

▸ EASY ◂

Let's start off nice and easy with three puzzles that are similar to the illustration puzzle. As a general hint, number the segments you see before starting, as in the illustration puzzle.

Puzzle 1

How many complete four-sided figures (squares and rectangles) are there in the diagram altogether? Note that a figure can be composed of smaller constituent figures.

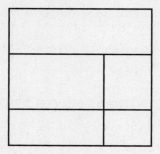

Puzzle 2

How many complete four-sided figures (squares and rectangles) are there in the following diagram altogether? As you know by now, a figure can be composed of smaller constituent figures.

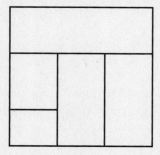

Puzzle 3

Let's do one more fairly easy puzzle. How many complete four-sided figures (squares and rectangles) are there in the following diagram altogether? A figure can be composed of smaller constituent figures.

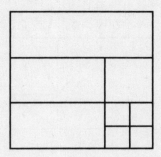

▶ MODERATELY HARD ◀

Now let's do a few triangle-counting puzzles.

Puzzle 4

How many complete triangles are there in the following diagram altogether? Note that a figure can be composed of smaller constituent figures.

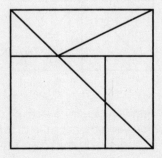

Puzzle 5

Let's do another one. How many complete triangles are there in the following diagram altogether? Note that a figure can be composed of smaller constituent figures.

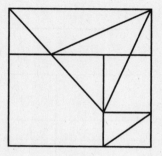

Puzzle 6

How many complete triangles are there in the following diagram altogether? Note that a figure can be composed of smaller constituent figures.

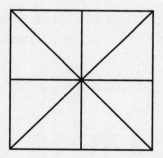

Embedding and rearranging figures is an old puzzle activity. Archimedes's game called the *loculus* is perhaps the best known one from the ancient past. It was a fourteen-piece puzzle forming a square from which it was possible to make different figures (animals, plants, and so on) by rearranging the pieces. An online version of the game can be found on the 4umi website at http://4umi.com/play/stomachion/pzl.php.

Puzzle 7

Let's change the diagram a bit! How many complete triangles are there in the following diagram altogether? Note that a figure can be composed of smaller constituent figures.

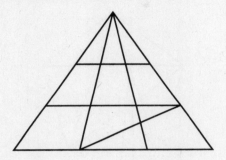

▶ DIFFICULT ◀

You will have to really sharpen your powers of observation for the last three puzzles in this section. Have fun!

Puzzle 8

How many complete four-sided figures (squares and rectangles) are there in the following diagram altogether? A figure can be composed of smaller constituent figures.

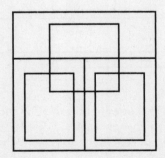

Puzzle 9

How many complete triangles are there in the following diagram altogether? Note that a figure can be composed of smaller constituent figures.

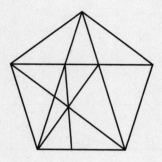

Puzzle 10

How many complete four-sided figures (squares and rectangles) are there in the following diagram altogether? A figure can be composed of smaller constituent figures.

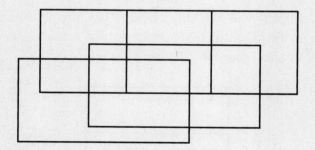

A jigsaw puzzle involves knowing how the bits and pieces of a picture are connected to form a whole shape or figure. Jigsaw puzzles were commercialized around 1760 by mapmaker John Spilsbury, who invented them to train children to discern shapes in maps.

Circles in Triangles

The next section also involves figure counting, but in a slightly different way. You will be asked to count how many triangles contain at least one circle. That's all there is to it. Let's do a very simple one for the sake of illustration.

▸ ILLUSTRATION ◂

In the following diagram, how many triangles, stand-alones and assembled, contain at least one circle? Note that a triangle can contain more than one circle in it.

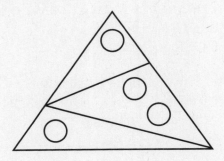

Let's number the diagram as in the previous puzzles for the sake of convenience. You must always keep in mind that there are stand-alone and assembled triangles in a diagram.

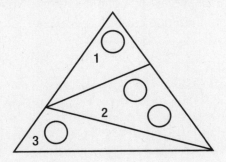

The stand-alones are 1, 2, and 3, and as you can see, each one has at least one circle in it—Triangle 2 has actually two of them. So far, therefore, three triangles contain at least one circle in them.

STAND-ALONES WITH AT LEAST ONE CIRCLE
1. Triangle 1: one circle
2. Triangle 2: two circles
3. Triangle 3: one circle

Now let's look at the assembled triangles.

ASSEMBLED TRIANGLES WITH AT LEAST ONE CIRCLE
4. Triangle 1 + 2: three circles
5. Triangle 1 + 2 + 3: four circles

So the answer is five triangles—that is, there are five triangles in the diagram that contain at least one circle in them.

▶ EASY ◀

Let's start with three easy puzzles.

Puzzle 11

In the following diagram how many triangles, stand-alones and assembled, contain at least one circle in them? Note that a triangle can contain more than one circle.

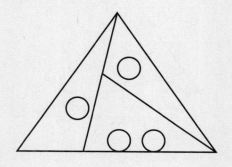

Puzzle 12

In the following diagram, how many triangles, stand-alones and assembled, contain at least one circle in them? Note that a triangle can contain more than one circle.

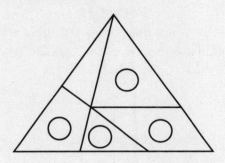

Puzzle 13

In the following diagram, how many triangles, stand-alones and assembled, contain at least one circle in them? Note that a triangle can contain more than one circle.

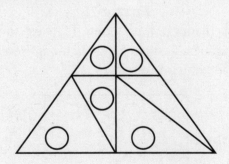

▶ MODERATELY HARD ◀

The level of difficulty has been increased a bit in the next four puzzles.

Puzzle 14

In the following diagram, how many triangles, stand-alones and assembled, contain at least one circle in them? Note that a triangle can contain more than one circle.

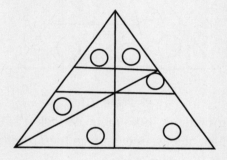

Puzzle 15

In the following diagram, how many triangles, stand-alones and assembled, contain at least one circle in them? Note that a triangle can contain more than one circle.

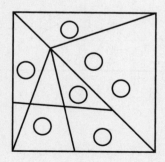

Puzzle 16

In the following diagram, how many triangles, stand-alones and assembled, contain at least one circle in them? Note that a triangle can contain more than one circle.

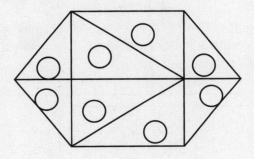

Puzzle 17

In the following diagram, how many triangles, stand-alones and assembled, contain at least one circle in them? Note that a triangle can contain more than one circle.

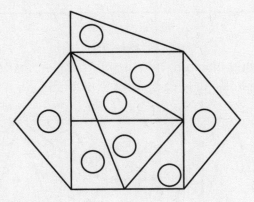

Tangram puzzles involve seeing how shapes can be combined to form larger figures. The origin of the tangram is uncertain, although most puzzle historians trace its invention to China. The puzzle consists of a square cut into five triangles, a smaller square, and a rhomboid. The challenge is how to reassemble them into different figures.

▸ DIFFICULT ◂

Are you ready to be challenged a bit more? Then check out these next puzzles.

Puzzle 18

In the following diagram, how many triangles, stand-alones and assembled, contain at least one circle in them? Note that a triangle can contain more than one circle.

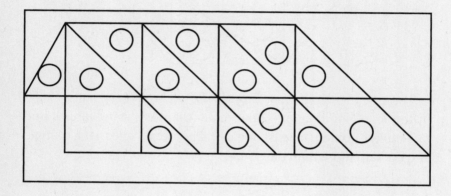

Puzzle 19

In the following diagram, how many triangles, stand-alones and assembled, contain at least one circle in them?

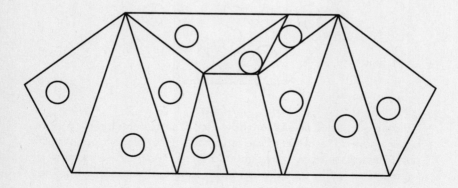

Puzzle 20

In the following diagram, how many triangles, stand-alones and assembled, contain at least one circle in them? Note that a triangle can contain more than one circle.

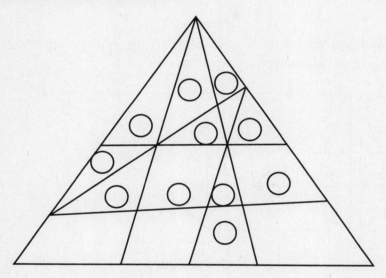

Have you noticed that the logo for Wikipedia is a globe consisting of jigsaw puzzle pieces? The claim is that the missing pieces are added regularly to complete the overall "knowledge picture"—a rather apt metaphor.

Figure-Counting Madness!

For the final five puzzles in this chapter anything goes. They vary in difficulty level, though. Some are harder than others. Good luck!

Puzzle 21

How many complete triangles, stand-alones and assembled, are there in the following diagram altogether?

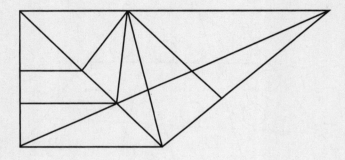

Puzzle 22

How many complete four-sided figures (squares and rectangles), stand-alones and assembled, are there in the following diagram altogether? This is an easy one, just to give you a bit of a break.

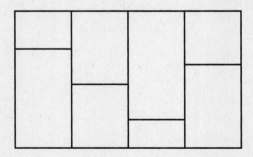

Puzzle 23

In the following diagram, how many complete four-sided figures (squares or rectangles), stand-alones and assembled, contain at least one circle in them? Note that a figure can contain more than one circle.

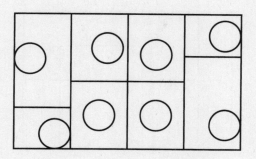

Puzzle 24

How many complete triangles, stand-alones and assembled, are there in the following diagram altogether?

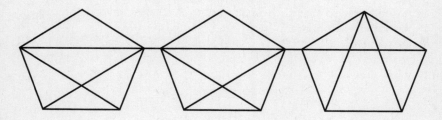

Puzzle 25

Let's end with a very simple puzzle, just to finish up in a logically reassuring way! How many complete four-sided figures (squares and rectangles), stand-alones and assembled, are there in the following diagram altogether?

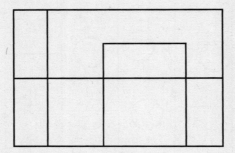

This chapter was really all about the perception of forms and patterns. These puzzles can be thought of as miniature models of our larger search for pattern. In this regard it is useful to quote the physicist Richard Feynman: "Nature uses only the longest threads to weave her patterns, so that each small piece of her fabric reveals the organization of the entire tapestry."

CHAPTER 2

Frameworks

The nice thing about doing a crossword puzzle is, you know there is a solution.
—STEPHEN SONDHEIM (B. 1930)

Puzzles that involve placing words in a crisscross fashion are a favorite pastime of many people. This type of puzzle is called a "framework." Frameworks are the kissing cousins of crosswords and acrostics. Whereas each of the letters in crosswords must be part of two words, vertically and horizontally, with no letters left over, in frameworks various patterns of letter crossing can occur, offering a different kind of challenge, depending on word length and place of occurrence of the letters in words. There are varying degrees of difficulty involved nonetheless, as you will see.

Basic Frameworks

The puzzles in this section constitute the basic type of framework puzzle. The challenge is to fit the given words into the diagram perfectly. That's all there is to it, but it is not as simple as it looks. Let's do an easy one together.

▶ ILLUSTRATION ◀

Insert these words into the framework. They will fit in only one way.

END
ENDURE
LOVE
NEW
TWO
WONDER

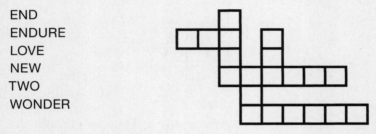

LOVE is the only four-letter word that will fit into the four-cell column in the framework. See it? Insert LOVE there immediately. With this insertion as a start, the other words are easily inserted as follows.

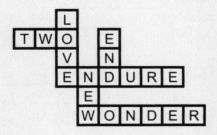

That's all there is to it. As you can see, you will have to do some trial and error in order to make the "word pieces" fit perfectly into the diagram, like pieces in a jigsaw puzzle. Have fun!

▶ EASY ◀

Let's start off with easy frameworks to get you warmed up!

Puzzle 1

Insert these five words into the framework. They will fit into the framework in only one way.

ART
BACK
BARBER
KNIT
LET

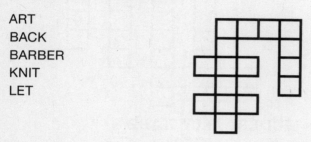

Puzzle 2

Insert these six words into the framework. They will fit into the framework in only one way.

ANOTHER
NOW
OVATION
POUR
TOO
TREND

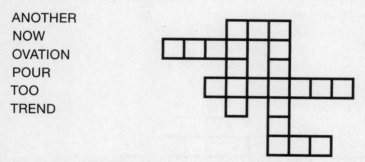

Frameworks, as mentioned, are the kissing cousins of crosswords. Both are very popular puzzles because they are addictive—you can't stop until you have solved them. Don't you agree?

Puzzle 3

Insert these seven words into the framework. They will fit into the framework in only one way.

BUS
CHILL
GRAPE
NIGHTLY
STILL
TEAM
TONIGHT

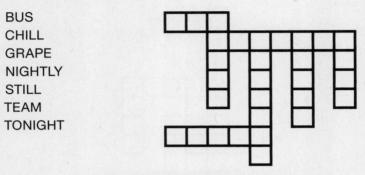

▶ MODERATELY HARD ◀

It's time for a few complicated frameworks!

Puzzle 4

Insert these eight words into the framework. They will fit into the framework in only one way.

ALIGN   IGNORANCE
CLAIM   MEMORANDUM
CLUE   STICK
DATA
FAMOUS

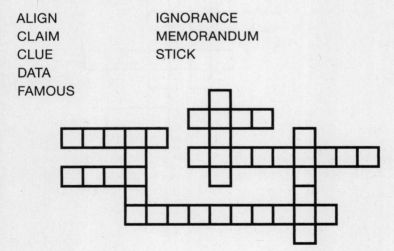

Puzzle 5

Insert these nine words into the framework. They will fit into the framework in only one way.

ABILITY
BAIT
CRY
LINE
MEETING
ROWING
SPEAK
TAPESTRY
YES

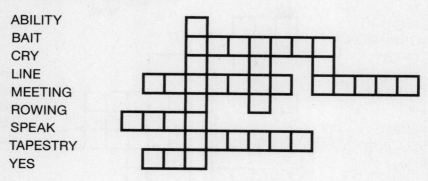

Puzzle 6

Insert these ten words into the framework. They will fit into the framework in only one way.

DETAIL
ENCODE
ENTICE
FOUR
LAVA
SISTER
SUNSHINE
TEST
TREE
TRUST

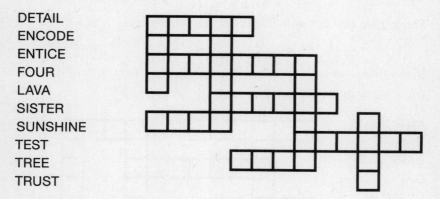

Puzzle 7

Insert these eleven words into the framework. They will fit into the framework in only one way.

ANCHOR
CHAMPION
EXACT
GOAL
IMAGINE
IT
LIGHT
MARKET
TEN
YEN
YET

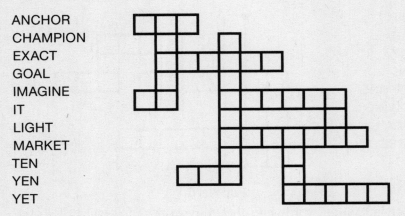

▶ **DIFFICULT** ◀

These next puzzles will give you a real challenge!

Puzzle 8

Insert these twelve words into the framework. They will fit into the framework in only one way.

ANTICIPATE
BALK
BARK
CAT
CLAMOR
ENTRANCE
FUN
KNIFE
LIP
LUCKY
PENSION
TRIVIAL

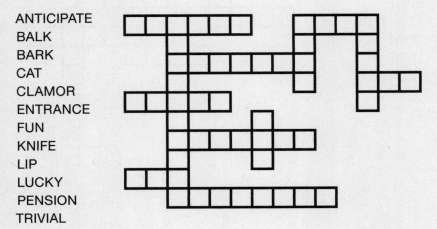

Puzzle 9

Insert these thirteen words into the framework. They will fit into the framework in only one way.

BOOK   EAT   THAT
BUS   GREAT   TIN
CAR   KNIGHT   TRUE
DOG   STEM
DOGMATIC   TESTOSTERONE

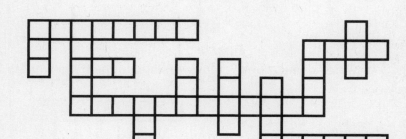

Puzzle 10

Insert these fourteen words into the framework. They will fit into the framework in only one way.

ASK   HER   TRIP
BETTERMENT   PUN   UNDER
CALM   RESTORATION
CHAT   RUG
DELIGHT   SMART
ENTRY   THOUGHT

Definition Frameworks

Definition frameworks are much more challenging overall than the puzzles in the previous section, because you are not given the words, only their definitions, in no particular order, although they are numbered consecutively.

▶ EASY ◀

Let's start with easy puzzles, just to get you familiarized with this type.

Puzzle 11

The four words defined by the clues will fit into the framework in only one way.

1. Opposite of love
2. Five plus five
3. A lot
4. It falls in winter

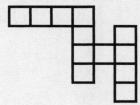

Puzzle 12

The four words defined by the clues will fit into the framework in only one way.

1. Cease moving
2. Attempt
3. Common greeting
4. Go away

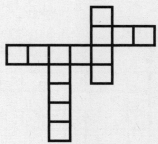

Puzzle 13

The five words defined by the clues will fit into the framework in only one way.

1. Small
2. Close-fitting
3. Type of adhesive
4. Opposite of down
5. Allow

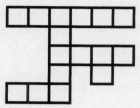

▶ MODERATELY HARD ◀

Are you ready for slightly more challenging puzzles?

Puzzle 14

The six words defined by the clues will fit into the framework in only one way.

1. Opposite of above
2. Opposite of ahead
3. Diagram, table
4. Move at a fast pace
5. At no time
6. Opposite of enemy

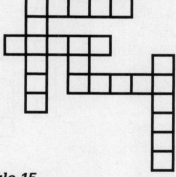

Puzzle 15

The six words defined by the clues will fit into the framework in only one way.

1. Clairvoyant
2. Exceptional, unusual
3. Morsel
4. Perhaps
5. Completely
6. Dine, consume

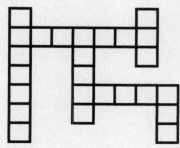

Puzzle 16

The seven words defined by the clues will fit into the framework in only one way.

1. Right, precise
2. Kitchen stove, range
3. Very great, utmost
4. Opposite of imaginary
5. An insect
6. Chum
7. Also

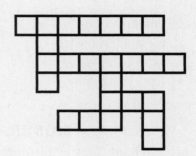

Puzzle 17

The seven words defined by the clues will fit into the framework in only one way.

1. Explosion
2. Opposite of found
3. Tip over
4. Romantic partner
5. Smooth, level
6. Asphalt
7. Renter, occupant

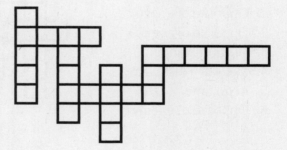

Crosswords have been "addictive" since they were invented in 1913 by an editor for *New York World*'s "Fun" section, Arthur Wynne. In the Broadway play *Puzzles of 1925*, there is a "crossword sanitarium" where those suffering from crossword addiction and obsession are confined.

▶ DIFFICULT ◀

It's time for a real challenge, as you will see with the next three puzzles!

Puzzle 18

The eight words defined by the clues will fit into the framework in only one way.

1. Seller, merchant
2. Aristocratic
3. Skill, aptitude
4. Flat eating surface

5. Woven container
6. Set of articles, equipment
7. Saliva
8. Choose

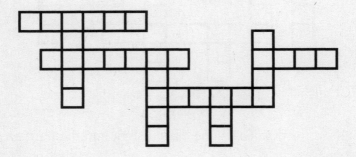

A principle in the puzzle world states that every puzzle has a flaw. The framework's flaw is that it allows no leeway for error. If you make an error along the way, you will simply have to start over from scratch.

Puzzle 19

The nine words defined by the clues will fit into the framework in only one way.

1. Permit
2. Opposite of harsh or severe
3. Bird home
4. With each other
5. Obtain

6. Protruding part of the face
7. Lion's cry
8. Opposite of closed
9. Nothing, zero

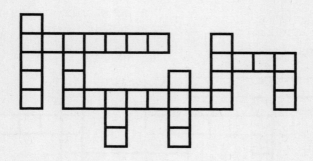

Puzzle 20

The ten words defined by the clues will fit into the framework in only one way.

1. The science of the mind
2. Utensil for eating soup
3. Move behind someone
4. Labor
5. Indecent

6. Tally of points in a game
7. Relax
8. Escape
9. Opposite of back
10. Offspring born together

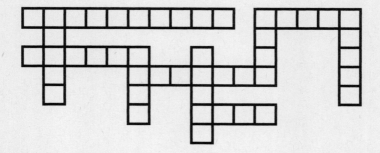

Letter Frameworks

After the tough nuts of the previous section, it is time for a logical respite. The following five puzzles will give you both the definitions and some of the letters of the words. They are not as simple as they might appear, though.

Puzzle 21

The following framework provides some of the letters of the crossing words. Can you complete the framework? The words are defined as follows, in no particular order.

1. Each
2. Place to live
3. Pile
4. A vessel

5. Calm
6. Opposite of bitter
7. Attempt

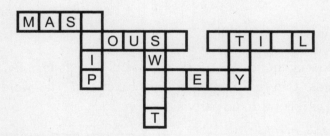

Frameworks involve connecting words in a similar way that pieces are put together in a jigsaw puzzle. By the way, did you know that the jigsaw puzzle became so popular that in 1909 the Parker Brothers company devoted an entire part of its factory to its production?

Puzzle 22

The following framework provides some of the letters of the crossing words. Can you complete the framework? The words are defined as follows, in no particular order.

1. Plus
2. Understandable
3. Container
4. Passion

5. Something missing
6. Encounter
7. Preceding

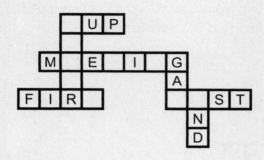

Puzzle 23

The following framework provides some of the letters of the crossing words. Can you complete the framework? The words are defined as follows, in no particular order.

1. Painting, for example
2. Cook
3. Popular sport
4. Aid
5. A chess piece
6. Exist
7. A cat, for example
8. Sleeveless garment

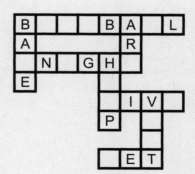

Puzzle 24

The following framework provides some of the letters of the crossing words. Can you complete the framework? The words are defined as follows, in no particular order.

1. Cheerful
2. Tie
3. A lot
4. Send
5. Team members
6. Hut
7. Avoid
8. Of particular kind

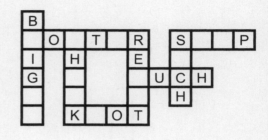

Puzzle 25

The following framework provides some of the letters of the crossing words. Can you complete the framework? The words are defined as follows, in no particular order. Note that there is a dark cell.

1. Response
2. Secluded place
3. Strong desire
4. Dinner
5. Provide
6. Move through water
7. Unit of length
8. Twelve months

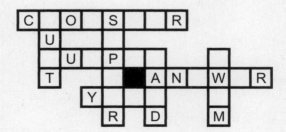

It is appropriate to finish off this chapter with the wise words about words by none other than Shakespeare: "Where words are scarce, they are seldom spent in vain."

CHAPTER 3

Box Puzzles

I thought boxes were the best toy. When my
parents got a new car, I ran to my mother
and said, "Did it come in a box?"
—COLIN ANGLE (B. 1967)

Containers such as boxes are essential for holding and protecting objects, goods, food, and anything that is packaged for sale or else preserved by people for various reasons. But boxes can also be used for puzzle purposes. This chapter will employ boxes to challenge your logic skills. The puzzles will require figuring out what's in certain boxes or matching box labels with contents. The last five puzzles in this chapter will also test your counting skills.

What's in the Boxes?

The classic type of box puzzle presents three boxes with wrong labels on them. You have to relabel them on the basis of logic alone, given certain information. Let's do one for the sake of illustration.

▶ ILLUSTRATION ◀

Three boxes, A, B, and C, contain fourteen billiard balls in total, colored blue or red. The boxes are labeled as shown, but the labels are wrong, because someone had switched the labels on all three boxes. Can you figure out the correct labels if someone draws out a blue ball from Box B?

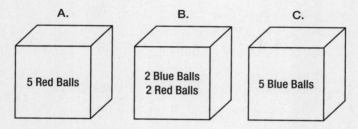

We know that Box B does not contain the two blue and two red balls, since it is mislabeled. So it has either the five red balls or the five blue balls. Because someone drew out a blue ball, we can now be sure that it contains the five blue balls. Let's show this as follows.

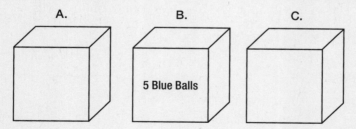

We know that A does not contain the five red balls, because of the wrong label, nor does it contain the five blue balls (since we just deduced that B does); so it contains the two blue and two red balls (by process of elimination).

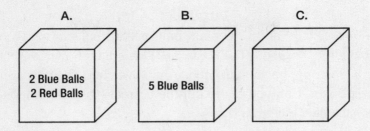

This means that the remaining five red balls are in Box C.

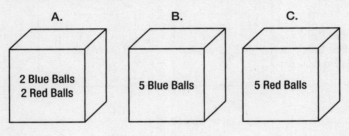

▶ EASY ◀

Let's do three more that are similar to the illustration puzzle, just to get started.

Puzzle 1

Three boxes, A, B, and C, contain five billiard balls in total, colored blue or red. The boxes are labeled as shown, but the labels are wrong, because someone had switched the labels on all three boxes. Can you figure out the correct labels if someone draws out a blue ball from Box A?

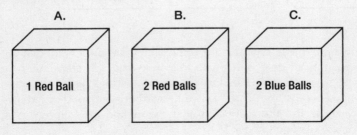

Puzzle 2

Three boxes, A, B, and C, contain nine billiard balls in total, colored blue, red, or green. The boxes are labeled as shown, but the labels are wrong, because someone had switched the labels on all three boxes. Can you figure out the correct labels if someone draws out a blue ball from Box A?

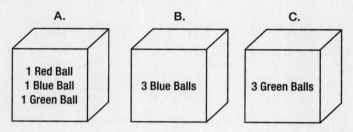

A.
1 Red Ball
1 Blue Ball
1 Green Ball

B.
3 Blue Balls

C.
3 Green Balls

Puzzle 3

Three boxes, A, B, and C, contain sixteen billiard balls in total, colored blue, red, and green. The boxes are labeled as shown, but the labels are wrong, because someone had switched the labels on all three boxes. Can you figure out the correct labels if someone draws out a green ball from Box B?

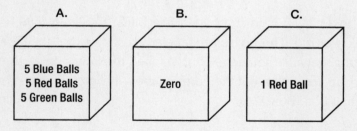

A.
5 Blue Balls
5 Red Balls
5 Green Balls

B.
Zero

C.
1 Red Ball

The puzzles in this chapter are reminiscent of something that former secretary of defense Donald Rumsfeld said: "There are known knowns; there are things we know we know. We also know there are known unknowns; that is to say we know there are some things we do not know. But there are also unknown unknowns—the ones we don't know we don't know."

▸ MODERATELY HARD ◂

Box logic is fun, isn't it? Try these slightly harder puzzles.

Puzzle 4

Three boxes, A, B, and C, contain nine billiard balls in total, colored blue, red, and green. The boxes are labeled as shown, but the labels are wrong, because someone had switched the labels on all three boxes. Can you figure out the correct labels if someone draws out three red balls from Box B?

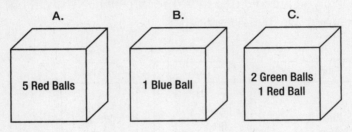

Puzzle 5

Three boxes, A, B, and C, contain fourteen billiard balls in total, colored red, green, and white. The boxes are labeled as shown, but the labels are wrong, because someone had switched the labels on all three boxes. Can you figure out the correct labels if someone draws out two red balls from Box C?

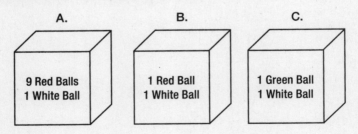

Puzzle 6

Three boxes, A, B, and C, contain ten billiard balls in total, colored red, green, and white. The boxes are labeled correctly this time but only indicate the colors of the balls within them, not the quantity of each colored ball. At the top of each box is a label indicating the total quantity of the balls in the box. For example, the "5 balls" label on Box A means that there are five balls inside, colored red and white. We do not know how many of each, though. Can you figure out the exact number of each of the colored balls within each box if you are told that there are three white balls in one of the boxes and two in another?

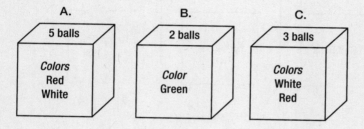

Since this chapter is all about boxes, let's talk about an interesting box. Have you ever heard of a box kite? It was invented by Australian Lawrence Hargrave in 1893. It is, as its name implies, a box-shaped kite with sides that are squares, rectangles, and triangles.

Puzzle 7

Let's do a puzzle similar to the previous one. Three boxes, A, B, and C, contain eleven billiard balls in total, colored blue, red, green, and white. The boxes are labeled correctly but only indicate the colors of the balls within them, not the quantity of each colored ball. At the top of the box is a label indicating the total quantity of the balls in the box. Can you figure out the exact number of each colored ball within each box if you are told that there are three blue, three red, and three white balls in total?

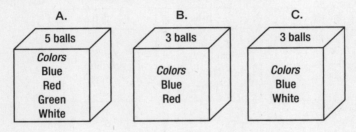

▶ DIFFICULT ◀

It's time for really challenging puzzles!

Puzzle 8

Three boxes, A, B, and C, contain twenty billiard balls in total, colored blue, red, green, and white. The boxes are labeled correctly but only indicate the colors of the balls within them, not the quantity of each colored ball. At the top of the box is a label indicating the total quantity of the balls in the box. Can you figure out the exact number of each colored ball within each box if you are told that there are only two red balls and five blue balls in total?

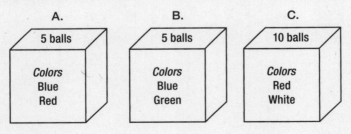

Puzzle 9

Three boxes, A, B, and C, contain eighteen billiard balls in total, colored blue, red, green, and white. The boxes are labeled correctly but only indicate the colors of the balls within them, not the quantity of each colored ball. At the top of the box is a label indicating the total quantity of the balls in the box. Can you figure out the exact number of each colored ball within each box if you are told that there are five red balls and seven green balls in total?

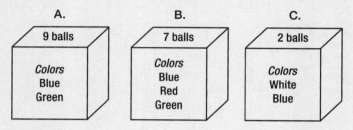

Puzzle 10

Okay, just one more. Three boxes, A, B, and C, contain fourteen billiard balls in total, colored blue, red, green, and white. The boxes are labeled correctly this time but only indicate the colors of the balls within them, not the quantity of each colored ball. At the top of the box is a label indicating the total quantity of the balls in the box. Can you figure out the exact number of each colored ball within each box if you are told that there are four red balls, two white balls, and five blue balls in total?

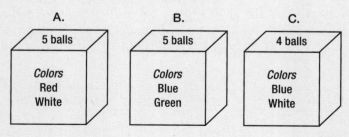

What's in the Boxes This Time?

The puzzles in this next section are a bit different from the previous ones, but the logic used is essentially the same. Let's do one together for the sake of illustration.

▸ ILLUSTRATION ◂

There is one coin hidden away in one of the three boxes, A, B, and C. The labels provide clues as to where it is. Can you locate it if you are told that two of the labels are true and the other false?

A.
The coin is
not in here

B.
The coin is
not in here

C.
The coin is
not in A

The labels on A and C say the same thing—namely, that the coin is not in A. So the two labels are either both true or both false. They cannot be both false, since there is only one false label. So they are both true. This means that the false label is the one on B (since A and C are true). Contrary to what it says—"The coin is not in here"—the coin is actually in B.

▸ EASY ◂

Confused? Let's start with a few easy ones so you can become somewhat familiar with the kind of logic needed here.

One of the most famous puzzles in box logic comes from Shakespeare's *The Merchant of Venice*. In the play, Portia's potential suitors must choose among three caskets composed of gold, silver, and lead. The one who chooses the right casket, containing Portia's portrait and a scroll, will win her hand in marriage.

Puzzle 11

There is one coin hidden away in one of the three boxes, A, B, and C. The labels provide clues as to where it is. Can you locate it if you are told that all the labels are true?

Puzzle 12

There is one coin hidden away in one of the three boxes, A, B, and C. The labels provide clues as to where it is. Can you locate it if you are told that all of the labels are false?

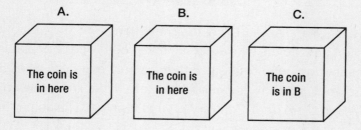

The game show *Let's Make a Deal* (starting in 1963), originally hosted by Monty Hall, exemplifies the kind of thinking required to solve the puzzles of this chapter. Contestants had to choose among three doors. One concealed the main prize and the other two concealed less valuable ones. This game show posed a statistical probability problem now well known in mathematics as the Monty Hall problem.

Puzzle 13

There is one coin hidden away in one of the three boxes, A, B, and C. The labels provide clues as to where it is. Can you locate it if you are told that two of the labels are true and the third one false?

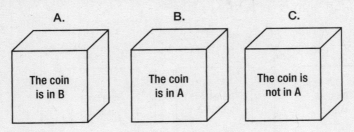

A. The coin is in B

B. The coin is in A

C. The coin is not in A

▸ MODERATELY HARD ◂

The search for the hidden coin is going to get a little more complex, logically speaking.

Puzzle 14

There is one coin hidden away in one of the three boxes, A, B, and C. The labels provide clues as to where it is. Can you locate it if you are told that two of the labels are false and one true?

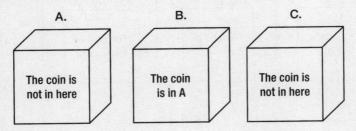

A. The coin is not in here

B. The coin is in A

C. The coin is not in here

Puzzle 15

There is one coin hidden away in one of the three boxes, A, B, and C. The labels provide clues as to where it is. Can you locate it if you are told that one of the labels is false and one is true, but we don't know if the third label is true or false?

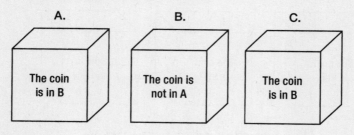

Puzzle 16

There is one coin hidden away in one of the three boxes, A, B, and C. The labels provide clues as to where it is. Can you locate it if you are told that the coin is not in C but that it is in a box with a false label on it?

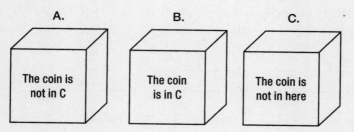

Puzzle 17

There is one coin hidden away in one of the three boxes, A, B, and C. The labels provide clues as to where it is. Can you locate it if you are told that two of the labels are true and one is false?

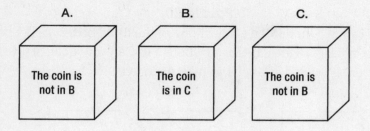

▸ DIFFICULT ◂

Try your hand at the next three challenging puzzles.

Puzzle 18

There is one coin hidden away in one of the three boxes, A, B, and C. The labels provide clues as to where it is. Can you locate it if you are told that there were two true labels and one false label? Also, we are told that the coin is in the box with the false label.

Puzzle 19

There is one coin hidden away in one of the three boxes, A, B, and C. The labels provide clues as to where it is. Can you locate it given that there is only one true label (and two false ones) and that the coin is in the box with the true label?

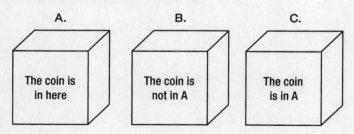

Puzzle 20

There is one coin hidden away in one of the three boxes, A, B, and C. The labels provide clues as to where it is. Can you locate it given that there is one false label and two true ones?

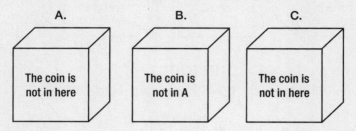

A. The coin is not in here

B. The coin is not in A

C. The coin is not in here

Box-Weighing Puzzles

The following five puzzles are somewhat different. You will be asked to distribute certain weights in three boxes in specific ways. They vary in difficulty level. Some are harder than others. Have fun!

Puzzle 21

Distribute the nine weights into the three boxes so that each box will have the same total weight. Some of the weights have already been inserted into the boxes as shown. Note that when they are empty the boxes weigh the same. All nine weights must be used once, and only once.

1 lb.	2 lbs.	3 lbs.	4 lbs.	5 lbs.	6 lbs.	7 lbs.	8 lbs.	9 lbs.

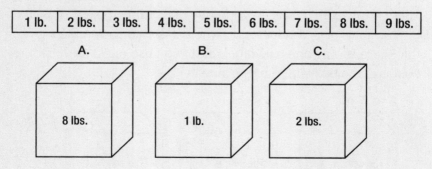

A. 8 lbs.

B. 1 lb.

C. 2 lbs.

Puzzle 22

Distribute the nine weights into the three boxes so that A's weight will equal the total weight of B and C combined: that is, A = B + C. Some of the weights have already been inserted into the boxes as shown. Note three things: (a) the empty boxes weigh the same at the start; (b) all nine weights have to be used; and (c) there are two 1-lb. weights.

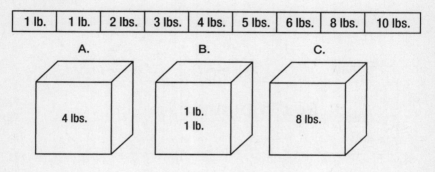

| 1 lb. | 1 lb. | 2 lbs. | 3 lbs. | 4 lbs. | 5 lbs. | 6 lbs. | 8 lbs. | 10 lbs. |

A. — 4 lbs.
B. — 1 lb. / 1 lb.
C. — 8 lbs.

Puzzle 23

Distribute the seven weights into the three boxes so that A and B will have only one weight each in them and when added together the total weight will equal the sum of the five weights in C alone— that is, A + B = C. One weight has been inserted already for you in A. All seven weights must be used once, and only once.

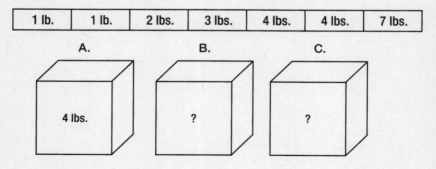

| 1 lb. | 1 lb. | 2 lbs. | 3 lbs. | 4 lbs. | 4 lbs. | 7 lbs. |

A. — 4 lbs.
B. — ?
C. — ?

Puzzle 24

Distribute the nine weights into the three boxes so that each box will weigh exactly the same. Here's how they are to be distributed (indicated on the top of each box): (a) Box A must have two weights; (b) Box B must have three weights; and (c) Box C must have four weights. Two of the weights have been inserted for you. All the weights have to be used once, and only once.

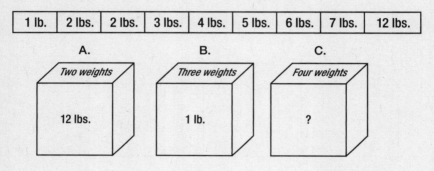

Puzzle 25

Distribute the seven weights into the three boxes so that B is twice the weight of A, and C is twice the weight of B. Two of the weights have been inserted for you. All of the weights must be used once, and only once.

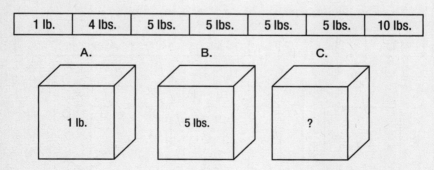

The kind of logic used in solving the puzzles in this chapter is based on deduction. It involves comparing things, eliminating possibilities, and reaching a single and undeniable conclusion.

CHAPTER 4

Math Puzzles

*As far as the laws of mathematics refer to
reality, they are not certain, and as far as they
are certain, they do not refer to reality.*
—ALBERT EINSTEIN (1879–1955)

For some of us the word "math" brings to mind images of problems in addition, subtraction, multiplication, division, fractions, and the like. Where's the fun in that? As Lord Byron once said: "I know that two and two make four and should be glad to prove it too if I could—though I must say if by any sort of process I could convert two and two into five it would give me much greater pleasure." Well, there is a lot of fun in math. Indeed, some of the oldest puzzles in existence are math puzzles. In this chapter your ability to reason both about numbers and with numbers will be put to the test.

Number Riddles

Riddles have been around since the dawn of history. Perhaps the oldest is the riddle of the Sphinx, which comes out of myth and ancient Greek drama. It asks: "What is it that walks on four at dawn, two at noon, and three at twilight?" The riddle is a metaphor for human beings, who crawl on all fours at the dawn of life (infancy), stand up when they grow up and walk on two feet (the "noon hour" of life), and require help walking with a cane at twilight (old age).

In this section we turn our attention to riddles about numbers. Let's do a very simple one together for the sake of illustration.

▸ ILLUSTRATION ◂

If you multiply any number by me, you will always get the same result—the number itself, which you multiplied by me! What number am I?

The answer is 1. Multiplying any number by 1 produces that number again: $1 \times 4 = 4$; $1 \times 86 = 86$; $1 \times 4{,}568 = 4{,}568$; and so on.

▸ EASY ◂

Number riddles are fun, aren't they? Let's start with three very simple ones.

Puzzle 1

If you divide any number by me, you will always get the same result—the number itself, that is, the number into which you divided me! What number am I?

Puzzle 2

I am a number less than 20 but greater than 11 that can be divided evenly by 5. What number am I?

Puzzle 3

I am a number less than 20. If you multiply me by 2, you will get a number that, if increased by 2, will produce the final result of 24. What number am I?

► MODERATELY HARD ◄

It's time for a few more challenging riddles!

Puzzle 4

If you multiply me by 11 and then subtract me (again) from that result, you will get 30. What number am I?

Puzzle 5

If you add me three times to a number less than 20, you will get a result that, when divided by 8, will produce me again! What number am I? By the way, I too am a number less than 20.

Puzzle 6

I am a number less than 10. If you multiply me by myself four times, you will get a result that, when divided by 64, will produce me again. What number am I?

Puzzle 7

Do you remember what a prime number is? It is a number greater than 1 that cannot be divided by any other number except itself and 1. Here's the riddle: I am a prime number less than 20. If you add me to the next highest prime number after me, you will get a result that, when divided by 5, will equal 6. What number am I?

> The cuneiform tablets of ancient cultures, such as the Sumerian and Babylonian ones, about 5,000 years ago, reveal that even the earliest civilizations had sophisticated number systems for carrying out business transactions, measurements, mathematics, and various scientific activities. Similar writings are found throughout ancient cultures.

Are you ready for three really challenging number riddles?

Puzzle 8

I am a prime number greater than 37 but less than 67. If you subtract 8 from me, you will get a result that, when divided by 17, equals another prime number. What number am I?

Puzzle 9

I am a prime number less than 23 and greater than 5. If you multiply me by myself and then subtract 2 from the result, you will get a prime number between 40 and 50. What number am I?

Puzzle 10

I am a number greater than 30 and less than 40. If you divide me by 3, you will get a number divisible by 6. What number am I?

Number Squares

Sudoku is a logic placement puzzle, solved by filling in a grid with digits or other symbols in a specific way. In this section you will be dealing with similar types of puzzles. You are given a set of numbers to insert into the cells of a square figure according to a set of rules. Let's do a simple one together for the sake of illustration.

▶ ILLUSTRATION ◀

Insert the following numbers into the nine cells of the square according to the following rules. Note that a number can be used more than once (if required), but must be used at least once.

0, 2, 3, 4, 5, 6, 7

RULES

1. The numbers in each row when added together produces the constant sum of 12.
2. The number 7 occurs twice in the cells of two opposite corners of the square.
3. The numbers 3 and 5 must occur in the other two corner cells, opposite each other, with 3 in a top corner cell and 5 in a bottom corner cell.
4. There is only one 4 in the square, and it occurs in a cell right above a 0.
5. There is only one 6 in the square, and it occurs in a cell right above a 7.

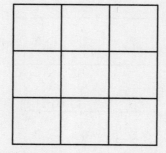

There are two ways in which to insert 7 in two corner cells (rule 2). Let's try one possibility. If it doesn't work out, we can always go back and try the other.

Applying rule 3 to the square, it is obvious that 3 goes in the top remaining corner and 5 in the bottom remaining corner.

7		3
5		7

The rest is now straightforward. The numbers in each row (but not each column) have to add up to 12 (rule 1). So the missing number in the top row is 2 (since $7 + 2 + 3 = 12$) and the missing one in the bottom row is 0 (since $5 + 0 + 7 = 12$).

7	2	3
5	0	7

According to rule 4, we can now put the 4 above the 0, and according to rule 5, the 6 above the 7. Missing from the middle row is 2, which will make the row add up to twelve ($2 + 4 + 6 = 12$).

7	2	3
2	4	6
5	0	7

▸ EASY ◂

Here are three puzzles at the same easy level of difficulty of the illustration puzzle.

Puzzle 11

Insert the following numbers into the nine cells according to the following rules. Note that a number can be used more than once (if required), but must be used at least once.

1, 2, 3, 4, 5, 6

RULES

1. The numbers in each column (but not necessarily in each row) when added together should produce the constant sum of 11.
2. There are three 5s in the square. One of them is in the top left corner cell. The other two 5s are in cells that are next to it and below it.
3. There is one 3, in one of the bottom corner cells of the square.
4. The 4 is in the middle cell.
5. In a cell to the right of one of the 5s is a 2.

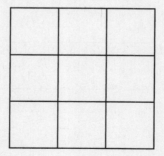

Puzzle 12

Insert the following numbers into the nine cells according to the following rules. Note that a number can be used more than once (if required), but must be used at least once.

0, 1, 2, 3, 4, 8, 9, 10

RULES

1. The numbers in each row and column when added together should produce the constant sum of 13—that is, the sum of the numbers in each row should equal 13, as should the sum of the numbers in each column.
2. The 8 is in the top left corner cell and the 3 in the top right corner cell.
3. Adding the numbers in the top left and bottom left corner cells together produces the sum of 12.
4. Adding the numbers in the other two corner cells together produces the sum of 3.

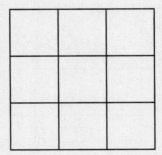

Puzzle 13

Insert the following numbers into the nine cells according to the following rules. Note that a number can be used more than once (if required), but must be used at least once.

2, 3, 4, 7, 8, 9, 10

RULES

1. The numbers in each row and column when added together should produce the constant sum of 20.
2. There are two 9s, which occur in the top row, and two 8s, which occur in the row just below. These occur consecutively—the 9 in one cell is followed immediately after it by the other 9, and the 8 is followed immediately after it by the other 8.
3. The 2 occurs in the top left corner cell, and the 10 in the bottom left corner cell.

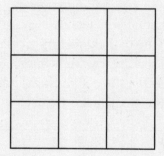

One of the most fascinating number squares of history is the magic square. In its original version it consisted of the first nine integers—1, 2, 3, 4, 5, 6, 7, 8, 9—arranged in a square pattern so that the sum of the numbers in each row, column, and diagonal is the same—15. This is called Lo Shu in China, from where it originated maybe as far back as 3000 B.C.E.

▸ MODERATELY HARD ◂

The next four puzzles raise the difficulty level a bit.

Puzzle 14

Insert the following numbers into the sixteen cells according to the following rules. Note that a number can be used more than once (if required), but must be used at least once.

0, 1, 3, 5, 6, 7, 8

RULES

1. The numbers in each row (but not necessarily in each column) when added together should produce the constant sum of 16.
2. The 7 is in the top left corner cell and the 1 in the bottom right corner cell.
3. There are three 3s, and they all occur in the top row.
4. Three of the 5s occur in the bottom row.
5. The other two 5s occur consecutively (one after the other) in the second row. One of these 5s is in a cell right below 7.
6. A 0 occurs in the second row, right after a 5.
7. An 8 occurs in a cell in the left-most column. It is followed immediately to its right by a 0.

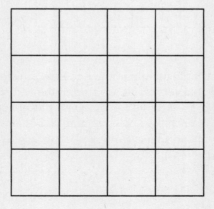

Puzzle 15

Insert the following numbers into the sixteen cells according to the following rules. Note that a number can be used more than once (if required), but must be used at least once.

1, 2, 3, 4, 6, 8, 9

RULES

1. The numbers in each column (but not necessarily in each row) when added together should produce the constant sum of 18.
2. There are four 4s in the square, two of which are in the two left-most cells of the top row.
3. There are two 2s in the square, which are in the two left-most cells of the bottom row.
4. There are four 3s in the square, two of which are in the top row and the other two in the right-most column—which has a total of three 3s.
5. There is one 9 and it occurs in the bottom right corner cell.
6. Of the three 8s in the square, one is in a cell in the bottom row. The other two 8s are in cells right above the two 2s.
7. The only 6 in the square is in a cell right below a 3.

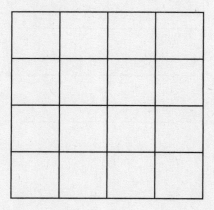

Puzzle 16

Insert the following numbers into the sixteen cells according to the following rules. Note that a number can be used more than once (if required), but must be used at least once.

1, 2, 3, 4, 7, 8, 9

RULES

1. The numbers in each row and each column when added together should produce the constant sum of 20.
2. Two of the corner cells contain a 7; the other two corner cells contain 1 and 4. The 4 is in the bottom right corner cell and the 1 in the bottom left corner cell.
3. There are two 3s in the top row.
4. Right below those 3s are the numbers 2 and 9, in that order.
5. The other two numbers in that row are 1 and 8. The 1 in that row is in a cell somewhere to the right of 2.
6. There is a 1 in a cell just below the only 9 in the square.

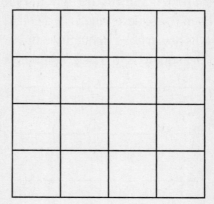

Puzzle 17

Insert the following numbers into the sixteen cells according to the following rules. Note that a number can be used more than once (if required), but must be used at least once.

1, 2, 3, 4, 5, 6, 7, 8, 9, 11

RULES

1. The numbers in each row and each column when added together should produce the constant sum of 23.
2. The four corner numbers are 2, 3, 5, and 11, but not necessarily in that order. In the corners, 2 is diagonally opposite to 3 and 5 to 11, and 11 is in the bottom right corner cell.
3. There are two occurrences of 2—one is in a cell in the top row, to the right of 5. The other numbers in the top row are 7 and 9 in consecutive order (one after the other).
4. The other 2 is in a cell in the second row right under the 7 in the top row. To its immediate left is the only 8 in the square. There is a 9 in a cell right below a 2.
5. In a cell right above 11, which occurs once in the square, is a 6.

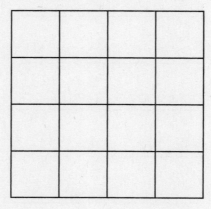

▸ DIFFICULT ◂

It's time to solve really challenging number square puzzles!

Puzzle 18

Insert the following numbers into the sixteen cells according to the following rules. Note that a number can be used more than once (if required), but must be used at least once.

1, 2, 3, 4, 5, 7, 8, 9

RULES

1. The last number in each row (the last cell on the right of a row) equals the sum of the first three numbers in that row.
2. A 3 occurs in the bottom right corner cell.
3. In the top two corner cells are the numbers 2 and 8 in some order.
4. In the cell right below the only 8 is the only 7. In the cell to the immediate left of the 7 is a 2. And in the cell to the immediate left of that 2 is a 1.
5. In the cell right below the only 4 is the only 5. In the cell to the immediate right of that 5 is a 1.

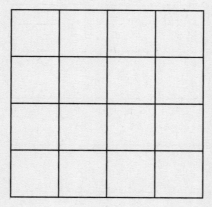

Puzzle 19

Insert the following three numbers into the sixteen cells according to the following rules. Note that a number can be used more than once (if required), but must be used at least once.

0, 1, 5

RULES

1. The numbers in the four corner cells when added together produce the sum of 20.
2. Adding the numbers in the top row produces the sum of 12. The same sum is produced by adding the numbers in the bottom row.
3. Adding the numbers in the left-most and right-most columns produces the same constant sum of 12.
4. Adding the numbers in the second column produces 2; adding the numbers in the column right after it also produces 2.

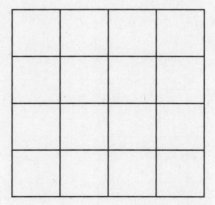

Renaissance mathematicians, such as Niccolò Tartaglia and Gerolamo Cardano, would often invent math puzzles to confuse each other and show off their own intellectual prowess, doing so publicly in the piazza—Italian for "public square."

Puzzle 20

Insert the following numbers into the sixteen cells according to the following rules. Note that a number can be used more than once (if required), but must be used at least once.

1, 2, 3, 5

RULES

1. The numbers in the four corner cells when added together produce the sum of 4.
2. Adding the numbers in the top row together produces the sum of 8. Similarly, adding the numbers in the bottom row together produces the same sum of 8.
3. Adding the numbers in the left-most column together produces the sum of 6. Similarly, adding the numbers in the right-most column together produces the same sum of 6.
4. The remaining cells contain 5s.

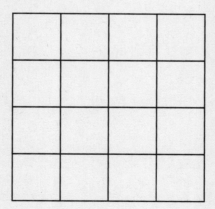

The ancient Chinese ascribed mystical properties to the magic square. Even today it is thought by many to provide protection against the evil eye when placed over the entrance to a room. Fortunetellers have also used magic squares to cast fortunes. In the late medieval period, amulets and talismans were designed with magic squares inscribed in them.

Number Mayhem

For the final five puzzles in this chapter anything goes. They vary in difficulty level, though. Some are harder than others. Good luck!

Puzzle 21

In the jumble of numbers in the following circle there are five and only five that add up to 25. There may be other combinations, made up of different sets of numbers (two, three, four), that add up to 25, but you must find the five that uniquely add up to 25. Can you find them? Note: the numbers can only be used once in the addition.

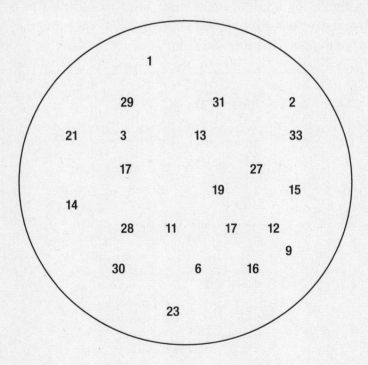

Puzzle 22

The arrangement of the numbers in each circle is based on a simple pattern. Knowing this, what is the missing number in the last circle?

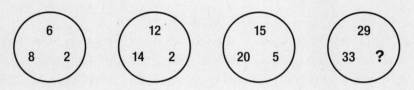

Puzzle 23

In the following array of digits there are two identical four-digit numbers whose individual digits add up to 34. They are read only from left to right. Can you find them?

2	3	5	2	7	7	5	4
1	8	8	9	9	0	2	3
6	3	3	0	5	6	6	9
8	6	2	1	4	9	5	1
8	7	8	8	9	9	9	2
3	4	5	3	4	9	5	6
1	2	4	5	6	3	2	1
8	9	0	5	4	1	9	2

78

Puzzle 24

The arrows show the initial and final numbers in the maze at the entrance and the exit of a specific numerical sequence whose sum is 23. Can you trace the path of numbers that leads from the 1 at the top to the 3 at the bottom that, when added together, produces the sum of 23?

7	1	1	3	2	4
7	2	0	1	0	5
7	8	3	9	8	5
4	4	4	0	8	7
7	8	9	1	2	8
0	9	8	2	2	3
6	5	7	8	2	9
4	5	7	8	1	9
1	0	3	6	1	5
5	5	5	5	1	5
5	9	8	6	3	5

Puzzle 25

For the final puzzle, let's do one last number riddle. Here it is: I am a number less than 40. I am three less than twice another number. When you add the two of us together, you will get 51. What number am I?

Number squares seem to have an aesthetic appeal. The German painter Albrecht Dürer (1471–1528) included a magic square in his famous 1514 engraving *Melencolia I*.

CHAPTER 5

Geometrical Figure Logic

Mathematics . . . would certainly not have originated if it had been known from the beginning that there is no exactly straight line in nature, no real circle, no absolute measure.
—FRIEDRICH NIETZSCHE (1844–1900)

The term "geometry" derives from the Greek words *geo* "earth" and *metrein* "to measure." This accurately described what the ancient geometers did. They were concerned with such problems as measuring the size of fields, laying out accurate right angles for the corners of buildings, and figuring out how shapes could be combined. Geometry is about literally "figuring out" things. In this chapter, you will be presented with geometrical figures that stand for numbers, or you might be asked to determine what figure is missing from a sequence of figures in some logical way. In other words, this chapter is about "geometrical figure logic," not about classic geometry puzzles, strictly speaking.

Geometrical Arithmetic

As the term "geometrical arithmetic" implies, the puzzles in this section are really arithmetic problems with geometrical figures. You are given a number of equations from which a figure is missing in the last equation. You have to select the missing one using logic. Let's do a simple one together for the sake of illustration.

▶ ILLUSTRATION ◀

Here are four equations with geometrical figures. Each figure stands for a specific number—that is, it has a specific numerical value. Find the missing figure.

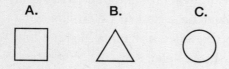

What's the missing figure?

A.   B.   C.

The answer is B. If you look carefully and compare the figures in the equations, you will see that the square stands for the number 4, the triangle for 3, and the circle for 1. Here are the numerical versions of the equations:

- $4 + 3 + 1 = 8$
- $4 - 1 = 3$
- $3 + 1 = 4$
- $4 - 1 + 3 \text{ (missing)} = 6$

So the missing figure is the triangle, which stands for 3.

▸ EASY ◂

Here are three puzzles similar to the illustration puzzle.

Puzzle 1

Here are four equations with geometrical figures. Each figure stands for a specific number—that is, it has a specific numerical value. Find the missing figure.

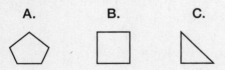

What's the missing figure?

A.   B.   C.

Puzzle 2

Here are four equations with geometrical figures. Each figure stands for a specific number—that is, it has a specific numerical value. Find the missing figure.

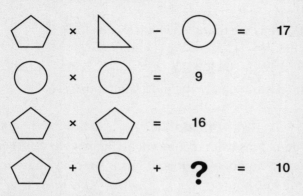

What's the missing figure?

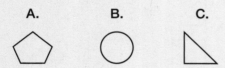

A.   B.   C.

Puzzle 3

Here are four equations with geometrical figures. Each figure stands for a specific number—that is, it has a specific numerical value. Find the missing figure.

□ + □ + ◯ + ◯ = 16

□ + □ + ◯ = 15

◺ + ◯ + ◯ + ◯ = 6

□ + ◯ + ◺ + **?** = 18

What's the missing figure?

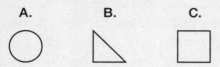

A.   B.   C.

▶ MODERATELY HARD ◀

The next four puzzles are a bit harder.

Puzzle 4

Here are four equations with geometrical figures. Each figure stands for a specific number—that is, it has a specific numerical value. Find the missing figure.

What's the missing figure?

A.   B.   C.   D.

The method of geometrical proof was developed by Pythagoras and systematized by Euclid in the *Elements* around 300 B.C.E. In that book, Euclid constructed an entire system of proof that we still use to this day.

Puzzle 5

Here are five equations with geometrical figures. Each figure stands for a specific number—that is, it has a specific numerical value. For this puzzle you will have to provide the missing number (after the equation sign) rather than a missing figure. Find the missing number.

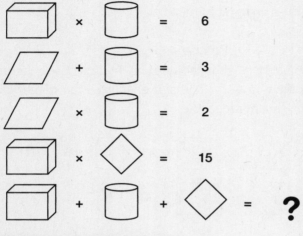

What's the missing number?

A.	B.	C.	D.
4	8	12	10

Practical geometry—geometry as a craft—flourished in ancient Egypt, Sumer, and Babylon. In the sixth century B.C.E., the Greek mathematician Pythagoras (c. 570–c. 495 B.C.E.) laid the cornerstone of theoretical geometry by transforming it into a logical discipline based on proving relations. Pythagoras admired geometry, not only on account of its great practicality, but also because of its tremendous intellectual value and beauty. By the way, in Pythagorean geometry, geometrical figures also stood for numbers, just like they do in the puzzles here.

Puzzle 6

Let's do a similar puzzle to the previous one. Here are five equations with geometrical figures. Each figure stands for a specific number—that is, it has a specific numerical value. Notice again that you will have to provide the missing number (after the equation sign) rather than a missing figure.

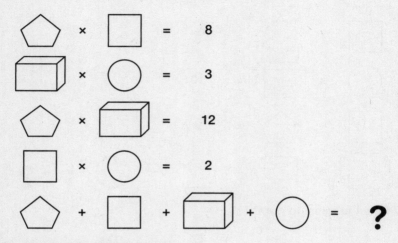

What's the missing number?

A.	B.	C.	D.
10	12	6	9

Puzzle 7

Let's do one more like the previous two. Here are five equations with geometrical figures. Each figure stands for a specific number—that is, it has a specific numerical value. Find the missing number.

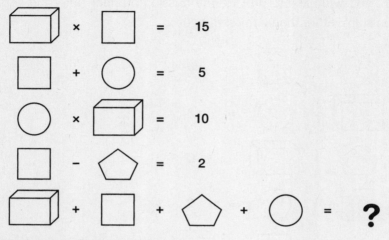

What's the missing number?

A.	B.	C.	D.
9	10	11	12

▶ DIFFICULT ◀

For the final three puzzles, the difficulty level is turned up a notch. No numbers are given, just figures. You will have to translate all the figures into numbers. Good luck!

Puzzle 8

Here are five equations with geometrical figures. Each figure stands for a specific number—that is, it has a specific numerical value. No figure in the puzzle has a numerical value greater than 9. Another clue: the circle stands for a number less than 3. Find the missing figure.

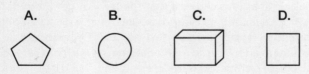

What's the missing figure?

A.	B.	C.	D.

Puzzle 9

Here are five equations with geometrical figures. Each figure stands for a different specific number—that is, it has a specific numerical value (different from the one it had in Puzzle 8). No figure in the puzzle has a numerical value greater than 10, and one of the figures stands for 1. Find the missing figure.

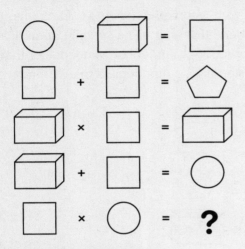

What's the missing figure?

A.   B.   C.   D.

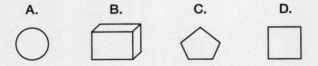

In the 500s B.C.E., Pythagoras showed that the laws of geometry followed logically from a limited number of axioms, such as: "A straight line is the shortest distance between two points." Pythagoras's approach was systematized by Euclid in the *Elements*, which has served as a basic textbook in geometry to the present day.

Puzzle 10

Here are five equations with geometrical figures. Each figure stands for a different specific number—that is, it has a specific numerical value. No figure in the puzzle has a numerical value greater than 12, and one of the figures stands for the number 2. Find the missing figure.

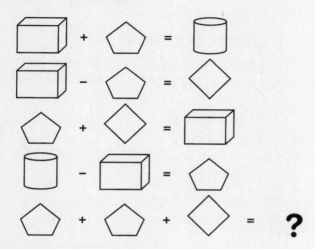

What's the missing figure?

A.   B.   C. D.

Figure Logic

The next section of puzzles requires visual-geometrical thinking. For the first three puzzles, you are given a sequence of four figures. On the basis of a pattern built into the sequence, you have to figure out what figure comes logically next. Let's do one simple puzzle together.

▶ ILLUSTRATION ◀

The following sequence of figures is based on a pattern—that is, each figure is placed in its position according to some sequential arrangement.

After figuring out the pattern, what figure should come next?

A.   B.   C.   D.

The answer is D, the heptagon (seven-sided figure). Each figure increases by one side from left to right: triangle (three sides)—square (four sides)—pentagon (five sides)—hexagon (six sides)—missing heptagon (seven sides).

Here are three similarly easy puzzles.

Puzzle 11

The following sequence of figures is based on a pattern—that is, each figure is placed in its position according to some sequential arrangement. What should the next figure be?

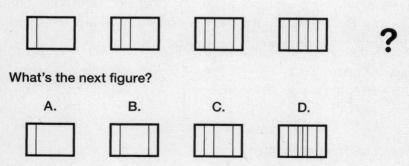

What's the next figure?

A.	B.	C.	D.

Puzzle 12

The following sequence of squares is based on a pattern—that is, each square follows in sequence according to some pattern. What should the next figure be?

What's the next figure?

A.	B.	C.	D.

Puzzle 13

The following sequence of circles is based on a pattern—that is, each circle follows in sequence according to some pattern. What should the next figure be?

What's the missing figure?

A.   B.   C.   D.

▶ MODERATELY HARD ◀

In the next set of puzzles, you will see a number above a figure that is connected to it in some way. You will have to figure out the missing number over the figure at the end of the set. A few hints are supplied to get you started.

Puzzle 14

The number above a specific figure is connected to it in some precise way. The figures are not laid out necessarily in any sequence. **Hint:** Look at the number of sides of a figure.

    6   3   4   5   **?**

What's the missing number?

    A.   B.   C.   D.

    5   7   2   4

Puzzle 15

The number above a specific figure is connected to it in some precise way. The figures are not laid out necessarily in any sequence. **Hint:** Look again at the number of sides of a figure, and then figure out the relation of the number above a figure to the number of sides.

8	8	6	10	?

What's the missing number?

A.	B.	C.	D.
8	10	12	16

Puzzle 16

The number above a specific figure is connected to it in some precise way. The figures are not laid out necessarily in any sequence. No more hints.

20	15	25	35	?

What's the missing number?

A.	B.	C.	D.
30	18	27	12

Puzzle 17

The number above a specific figure is connected to it in some precise way. The figures are not laid out necessarily in any sequence.

| 6 | 3 | 4 | 5 | **?** |

What's the missing number?

A.	B.	C.	D.
4	5	9	2

▶ DIFFICULT ◀

In the last three puzzles there will be two figures in the same position with a number above them. That number is connected to both those figures, not just one!

Puzzle 18

The number above each pair of figures is connected to them in some specific way. The figures are not laid out necessarily in any sequence.

| 7 | 12 | 10 | 8 | **?** |

What's the missing number?

A.	B.	C.	D.
12	9	8	10

Puzzle 19

The number above each pair of figures is connected to them in some specific way. The figures are not laid out necessarily in any sequence.

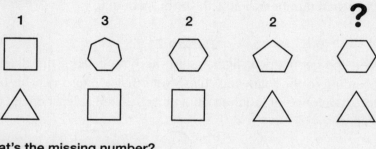

What's the missing number?

A.	B.	C.	D.
3	2	1	4

Puzzle 20

The number above each pair of figures is connected to them in some specific way. The figures are not laid out necessarily in any sequence.

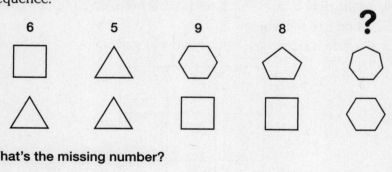

What's the missing number?

A.	B.	C.	D.
9	10	7	12

Geodoku

The final five puzzles of this chapter are a version of the placement principle in puzzles such as Sudoku—using geometrical figures rather than numbers, hence the term "geodoku."

Puzzle 21

Insert the geometrical figures into the nine cells of the diagram according to the following rules. Note that a figure can be used more than once (if required), but must be used at least once.

PLACEMENT RULES
1. There are exactly three circles, three squares, and three triangles in the diagram.
2. There are no circles in the corner cells.
3. In the left-most column, a circle is between a square above it and a square below it.
4. In the right-most column, a square is between a triangle above it and a triangle below it.
5. A circle is between a square and a triangle in two of the rows.

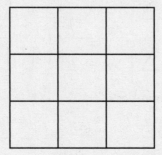

Puzzle 22

Insert the geometrical figures into the nine cells of the diagram according to the following rules. Note that a figure can be used more than once (if required), but must be used at least once.

PLACEMENT RULES

1. The only pentagon is placed in the middle cell of the diagram.
2. There are two circles. One is in the cell right above the pentagon. The other circle is somewhere in the bottom row.
3. There are three triangles in total. One is in the top right corner cell. Another one is in the top row as well.
4. There are three squares in total. One is in the bottom left corner cell, and another one is right above it in the same column.
5. There is a triangle in the bottom row in a cell to the immediate right of a square.

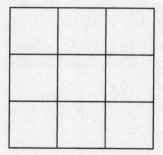

Puzzle 23

Insert the geometrical figures into the sixteen cells of the diagram according to the following rules. Note that a figure can be used more than once (if required), but must be used at least once.

PLACEMENT RULES

1. There are two circles in total, one in the top left corner cell and the other in the bottom right corner cell.
2. The top right corner cell contains the only square figure in the diagram; the remaining corner cell contains a triangle.
3. There are four pentagons in the square. One is in a cell to the immediate left of a circle, a second one is in a cell to the immediate right of a circle, a third is in a cell right below one of the circles, and the fourth one is in a cell just above the other circle.
4. In a cell below the square is a hexagon. Another hexagon is in a cell to the immediate left of the square. A third hexagon is in the bottom row to the immediate right of a triangle. The fourth and final hexagon is somewhere in the left-most column.
5. The remaining four cells contain triangles.

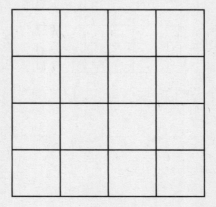

Puzzle 24

Insert the geometrical figures into the sixteen cells of the diagram according to the following rules. Note that a figure can be used more than once (if required), but must be used at least once.

PLACEMENT RULES

1. There are four circles, all of them placed in the four cells of one of the rows.
2. There are four pentagons, all of them placed in the four cells of another row, but below the circles somewhere.
3. In two of the cells below the pentagon row are two of the four square figures. The other two are in the bottom row.
4. The single hexagon is in the bottom right corner cell. There is a triangle in the cell to its immediate left, and there is a triangle in the cell just above it.
5. The remaining triangle is just below one of the pentagons.
6. The remaining cells are filled with squares.

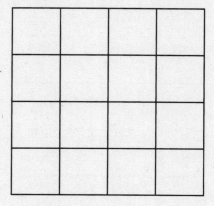

Puzzle 25

Insert the geometrical figures into the sixteen cells of the square according to the following rules. Note that a figure can be used more than once (if required), but must be used at least once.

PLACEMENT RULES

1. Three of the four corner cells contain a square; the other corner cell contains the only hexagon. There are three squares in total.
2. There are two circles in the top row in cells between two squares. The other two circles are to the immediate right (in separate cells, of course) to the third square.
3. There are four triangles. Two of them are in cells in the left-most column; the other two are in cells in the right-most column.
4. The remaining cells are filled with pentagons.

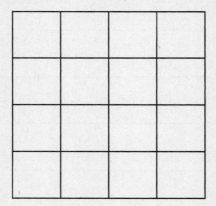

CHAPTER 6

Cryptarithms and Alphametics

Arithmetic is where the answer is right and everything is nice and you can look out of the window and see the blue sky—or the answer is wrong and you have to start all over and try again and see how it comes out this time.
—CARL SANDBURG (1878–1967)

Two of the more interesting, and challenging, puzzles invented in the twentieth century are called cryptarithms and alphametics. The term "cryptarithm" was originally coined by M. Vatriquant in the May 1931 issue of the Belgian puzzle magazine *Sphinx*. The real creator is generally believed to have been Sam Loyd, an American puzzlemaker. In 1924, another puzzlemaker, the Englishman Henry Dudeney, came up with a version in which he replaced all the numbers in a problem with letters that make up real words. This is now called "alphametic." The two terms are often used synonymously, but there is a difference, as you will see in this chapter, which is all about "cryptarithmetic."

Cryptarithms

A cryptarithm is a puzzle in which some or all of the digits in an addition, subtraction, division, or multiplication problem have been deleted. The goal is to reconstruct the numerical layout by deducing the missing numbers. This requires examining the various arrangements and locations of the given numbers and a basic understanding of how mathematical operations are carried out. Let's do a very simple one together for the sake of illustration.

▶ ILLUSTRATION ◀

Here is an addition problem from which certain digits have been deleted, shown by the question marks. Reconstruct the actual problem.

```
        ?   3
    ?   5   6
+           ?
_____
    4   8   1
```

Look at the right-most column. It can be represented as follows: $3 + 6 + ? = 1$. The only possibility for the question mark is 2, which means that there will be a carryover of 1, since $3 + 6 + 2 = 11$. Let's insert the 2 in the layout.

```
        ?   3
    ?   5   6
+           2
_____
    4   8   1
```

Carrying over the 1 to the next column we can see that:

1 (carryover) + ? + 5 = 8

The only possibility for the question mark is: $1 + 2 + 5 = 8$. There is no other digit that will work, as you can confirm by trying out different possibilities yourself. Let's insert this 2 in the layout.

```
        2  3
    ?   5  6
+          2
   ─────────
    4   8  1
```

Since there is no carryover in the last column, it is obvious that the missing digit is a 4, which is carried down below the line.

```
        2  3
    4   5  6
+          2
   ─────────
    4   8  1
```

▶ EASY ◀

Let's start with three easy addition problems.

Puzzle 1

Here is an addition problem from which certain digits have been deleted, shown by the question marks. Reconstruct the actual problem.

```
    ?  1  3
+   2  ?  ?
   ─────────
    8  5  8
```

Puzzle 2

Here is another addition problem from which certain digits have been deleted, shown by the question marks. Reconstruct the actual problem.

```
       4  1
    9  ?  ?
+   ?  1  6
   ─────────
 ?  0  7  5
```

Puzzle 3

Here is another addition problem from which certain digits have been deleted, shown by the question marks. Reconstruct the actual problem.

```
      ?  0  ?
      3  2  ?  5
  +   ?  4  5  1
  ─────────────
  1   0  2  6  5
```

▶ MODERATELY HARD ◀

The next section contains subtraction and multiplication cryptarithms. These are a bit harder than the previous ones.

Puzzle 4

Here is a subtraction problem from which certain digits have been deleted, shown by the question marks. Reconstruct the actual problem.

```
      4  ?  ?
  −   ?  9  6
  ───────────
      2  9  1
```

Puzzle 5

Here is another subtraction problem from which certain digits have been deleted, shown by the question marks. Reconstruct the actual problem.

```
      8  ?  0  0
  −   ?  5  ?  ?
  ──────────────
      3  2  2  2
```

Puzzle 6

Here is a multiplication problem completely laid out from which certain digits have been deleted, shown by the question marks. Reconstruct the actual problem.

```
      1  ?  0
  ×      8  ?
  ─────────────
      1  ?  0
   ?  ?  0
  ─────────────
   9  ?  2  0
```

Puzzle 7

Here is another multiplication problem completely laid out from which certain digits have been deleted, shown by the question marks. Reconstruct the actual problem.

```
         5  ?  ?
  ×         4  ?
  ────────────────
      ?  6  ?  5
   ?  1  ?  0
  ────────────────
   2  3  ?  2  ?
```

Sam Loyd (1841–1911) was, as mentioned, the likely person who invented cryptarithms. He was trained as an engineer, but in 1878, Loyd put together a compilation of chess puzzles that became so commercially successful that he decided to become a professional puzzlemaker from then on. He produced over ten thousand challenging puzzles in his lifetime, most of which continue to baffle solvers today.

► DIFFICULT ◄

The next three puzzles will really test your arithmetical logic skills. Good luck!

Puzzle 8

Here is a division problem from which certain digits have been deleted, shown by the question marks. Reconstruct the actual problem.

```
              1   ?   2
        ┌─────────────────
  2   ? │ 2   3   4   ?
        │ 2   ?
        │ ─────────
        │     ?   6
        │     4   ?
        │     ─────────
        │         0
```

Puzzle 9

Here is another division problem from which certain digits have been deleted, shown by the question marks. Reconstruct the actual problem.

```
              ?   5   ?
        ┌─────────────────
  1   2 │ 5   ?   ?   0
        │ ?   8
        │ ─────────
        │     6   ?
        │     6   0
        │     ─────────
        │         ?   0
        │         6   ?
        │         ─────────
        │             0
```

Puzzle 10

Here is an addition problem from which certain digits have been deleted, shown by the question marks. Reconstruct the actual problem.

```
      5  ?  5
   2  ?  5  ?
?  ?  5  1  3
+ ?  0  2  6  5  ?
------------------
1  6  9  8  1  9
```

Alphametics

The reasoning process involved in solving an alphametic is similar to that used in solving a cryptarithm. Unlike a cryptarithm, however, each digit has been replaced by a specific letter, as part of actual words. You are required to reconstruct the original numerical layout. Let's do a very simple one together.

▸ ILLUSTRATION ◂

Solve the following addition alphametic. To make sure that you do not get alternative answers, you will be provided with the value of one or more of the letters throughout. For this puzzle, D = 3 and I = 2.

```
      D  O
+  D  I  D
----------
   D  A  D
```

Let's start by putting D = 3 in the layout.

```
        3   O
  +  3   I   3
  _____
     3   A   3
```

The only possible digit in the right-most corner for the letter O is 0, since only $0 + 3 = 3$. Let's put this in the layout.

```
        3   0
  +  3   I   3
  _____
     3   A   3
```

We are told that I = 2, so let's put this in the layout.

```
        3   0
  +  3   2   3
  _____
     3   A   3
```

Clearly, A = 5.

```
        3   0
  +  3   2   3
  _____
     3   5   3
```

▶ EASY ◀

To get started, here are three easy alphametics.

Puzzle 11

Solve the following addition alphametic. For this puzzle, A = 3 and I = 6.

```
        I   T
  +     A   T
  _____
     S   E   E
```

Puzzle 12

Solve the following addition alphametic. For this puzzle, A = 3 and L = 2.

```
    A  L  M
+   L  A  M
_____
    E  E  L
```

Puzzle 13

Solve the following addition alphametic. For this puzzle, A = 3, E = 5, and S = 9.

```
    A  L  L
+   S  E  E
_____
    T  R  E  E
```

▶ MODERATELY HARD ◀

The next four puzzles are subtraction alphametics, making them a little harder to solve.

Puzzle 14

Solve the following subtraction alphametic. For this puzzle, A = 5 and E = 1.

```
    A  R  E
-      O  R
_____
    B  E  E
```

Henry Dudeney (1857–1930), the inventor of the alphametic, started creating puzzles at the age of nine, publishing them in a local paper under the pseudonym of "Sphinx." His collection of puzzles, *Amusements in Mathematics* (1917), provides many challenging puzzles.

Puzzle 15

Solve another subtraction alphametic. This alphametic uses an abbreviation (XXL). For this puzzle, G = 3 and X = 5.

```
  L A V A
- X X L
---------
  G L E E
```

Puzzle 16

Solve the following subtraction alphametic. One of the words, LAIT, is the French word for "milk." For this puzzle, I = 0, L = 1, and N = 6.

```
  T A I L
- L A I T
---------
  M O O N
```

Puzzle 17

Solve another subtraction alphametic. For this puzzle, O = 2 and W = 3.

```
  N O O N
-   W O N
---------
    S E E
```

It was J.A.H. Hunter, a puzzlemaker himself, who first used the word "alphametic" to distinguish it from a cryptarithm, because the letters replacing the numbers in it formed actual words—hence, alphabet + arithmetic = alphametic.

▶ DIFFICULT ◀

The next three alphametics are much harder than the previous ones. Good luck!

Puzzle 18

Solve the following addition alphametic. For this puzzle, D = 1, E = 2, and K = 4.

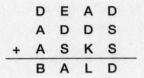

```
    D  E  A  D
    A  D  D  S
+   A  S  K  S
─────────────
    B  A  L  D
```

Puzzle 19

Solve the following subtraction alphametic. For this puzzle, A = 4 and O = 9.

```
    B  E  E  R
 −     B  R  O
─────────────
    C  A  R  E
```

Puzzle 20

The layout of the next puzzle has both digits and letters. Needless to say, each letter stands for one and only one digit. Reconstruct the actual layout.

```
    5  B  A  2  B
    C  2  B  B  2
+   C  5  2  5  5
────────────────
    A  A  9  A  A
```

Missing Symbols

The five puzzles in this section use arithmetical symbols, such as the plus sign (+), the subtraction sign (−), and so on. You will have to figure out which signs are missing in order to reconstruct the layout of a problem. The puzzles vary in difficulty level. Some are harder than others.

As an easy illustration, look at the following problem. Reconstruct it by replacing the question marks with the correct symbols. You can only use the four basic mathematical symbols (+, −, ×, and ÷).

$$(6 \; ? \; 8) \; ? \; 3 = 11$$

The answer is:

$$(6 + 8) − 3 = 11$$

Trying out other symbols will not lead to the 11 on the right side of the equation.

Puzzle 21

Replace each question mark with one of the four basic mathematical symbols (+, −, ×, and ÷) to reconstruct the layout. One of the symbols is supplied for you.

$$4 \; ? \; 5 \; ? \; 6 = 5 \times 3$$

Puzzle 22

Replace each question mark with one of the four basic mathematical symbols (+, −, ×, and ÷) to reconstruct the layout.

$$2 \; (23 \; ? \; 3) \; ? \; 40 = 0$$

Puzzle 23

Replace each question mark with one of the four basic mathematical symbols (+, −, ×, and ÷) to reconstruct the problem. One of the symbols is supplied for you.

$$(5 \; ? \; 6) \div 10 = 7 \; ? \; 4$$

Puzzle 24

Replace each question mark with one of the four basic mathematical symbols (+, −, ×, and ÷) to reconstruct the problem.

$$2 \; ? \; 2 \; ? \; 2 \; ? \; 2 \; ? \; 2 = 9 \; ? \; (4 \; ? \; 3)$$

Puzzle 25

Replace each question mark with one of the four basic mathematical symbols (+, −, ×, and ÷) to reconstruct the layout.

$$(99 \; ? \; 3) \; ? \; 7 = 4 \; ? \; 10$$

In 1893, Loyd and Dudeney started a correspondence. But Dudeney soon became upset with his American counterpart, breaking off relations after he started suspecting Loyd of stealing his ideas.

CHAPTER 7

River-Crossing Puzzles

You cannot step into the same river twice.
—HERACLITUS (535–475 B.C.E.)

Aclassic problem in logic is called the river-crossing puzzle. You have probably come across it at some point. It goes somewhat like this:

> *A traveler comes to a riverbank with a wolf, a goat, and a head of cabbage. He sees a boat that he can use for crossing over to the other bank, but to his dismay he notices that it can carry no more than two—the traveler himself and just one other. As the traveler knows, if left alone together on either bank, the goat will eat the cabbage and the wolf will eat the goat. The wolf does not eat cabbage. How does the traveler transport his animals and his cabbage to the other side intact in a minimum number of trips?*

This is the kind of puzzle you will encounter in this chapter, in various versions and variations. Have fun!

The Traveler's Dilemma

The basic river-crossing problem can be called the "traveler's dilemma" puzzle, since it involves a traveler having to make decisions as to how transport animals and things across a river with one boat with limited seating capacity.

The previous puzzle is the classic one, so let's go through it together for the sake of illustration.

▶ ILLUSTRATION ◀

Obviously, the traveler has to start with the goat; otherwise, if he starts by taking across the cabbage first, the wolf will be alone with the goat and eat it. Similarly, if he starts by taking the wolf first, then the goat is left to eat the cabbage. So let's set up the back-and-forth trips systematically.

- The traveler takes his first trip across the river to the other bank taking the goat with him, leaving the wolf and cabbage safely alone on the original side.
- When he is on the other bank, he drops off the goat, and for his second trip he goes back alone to the original side.
- On that side, he can then pick up either one—the wolf or the cabbage. It doesn't matter, since the final result (the number of trips required) will not change. Let's go with the wolf. Thus, for his third trip, he goes across to the other bank with the wolf on board.
- On the other side he drops off the wolf, but goes back with the goat; otherwise, the wolf would eat the goat. So on his fourth trip—back to the original side—he has the goat as a passenger.
- Once back on the original side, he drops off the goat, picks up the cabbage, and with it embarks on his fifth trip—to the other bank.
- When there, he drops off the cabbage, leaving it harmlessly with the wolf. He then goes back to the original side alone. This is his sixth trip across the river.

- When he gets back to the original side, he picks up the goat and goes over to the other side with it. When he gets there, he has the wolf, goat, and cabbage, intact, and thus he can continue with his journey.

As you can see, seven total trips, back and forth, were required to resolve the dilemma. There are other ways to count the number of trips, such as using round trips or back-and forth trips as units. For the sake of consistency, in the chapter we will count each trip, whether over or back, as a separate trip. That's how the answers will be explained at the back of the book.

▸ EASY ◂

For the puzzles in this section, the scenario is the same as it is in the illustration puzzle—a traveler comes to a riverbank and has to take certain animals and things to the other side intact. The traveler sees that the boat has limited seating.

Puzzle 1

Let's start very easily. The traveler has to take across two wolves and one goat. The boat can only carry two—himself and one other. If left on either bank alone with the goat, either wolf would eat the goat. What is the least number of trips in total (not round trips) needed by the traveler to get them all across safely and soundly and continue with his journey?

Puzzle 2

For this puzzle, the traveler is a young woman who has to take across one wolf and two goats. The boat can only carry two— herself and one other. If left on either bank alone, the wolf would eat either goat. What is the least number of trips in total (not round trips) needed by the traveler to get them all across safely and soundly and continue with her journey?

Puzzle 3

This time, the same traveler has to take across one goat and two heads of cabbage. The boat can only carry two—herself and one other. Again, if left on either bank alone, the goat would eat either cabbage. What is the least number of trips in total (not round trips) needed by the traveler to get them all across intact and continue with her journey?

▶ MODERATELY HARD ◀

It is time to raise the difficulty level a bit.

Puzzle 4

This time, the male traveler has to take across a wolf, a goat, and two heads of cabbage. The new boat can carry himself and only one other animal (wolf or goat), but can hold himself and the two cabbages. Again, if left on either bank without the traveler, the wolf will eat the goat, and the goat will eat either or both of the two cabbages. What is the least number of trips in total (not round trips) needed by the traveler to get them all across intact and continue with his journey?

Puzzle 5

The female traveler has to take across a wolf, two goats, and two heads of cabbage. The boat can seat three this time—herself and two others. You know the situation by now, so no need to repeat it here. What is the least number of trips in total needed by the traveler to get them all across intact and continue with her journey?

The river-crossing puzzle is attributed to the famous English scholar and ecclesiastic, Alcuin (C.E. 735–804), who became an adviser to the Holy Roman Emperor Charlemagne in 782.

Puzzle 6

The female traveler this time has to take across two wolves, two goats, and two heads of cabbage. The boat can seat three—herself and two others. You know the situation, so no need to repeat it here. What is the least number of trips in total (not round trips) needed by the traveler to get them all across safely and soundly and continue with her journey?

Puzzle 7

The male traveler comes to the riverbank with an ogre, a wolf, a goat, and a head of cabbage. The boat can carry only three—the traveler himself and two others. As the traveler knows, if left alone together on either bank, without his presence, the ogre will eat the wolf, the wolf will eat the goat, and the goat will eat the cabbage. The ogre does not eat cabbage or goats. And the goat does not eat ogres, of course. What is the least number of trips in total (not round trips) needed by the traveler to get them all across intact and continue with his journey?

▶ DIFFICULT ◀

The next three puzzles are labeled as "difficult," not because they are more complicated than the previous ones, but because they might vary a bit from them. Once you have grasped the logic behind the river-crossing genre, there really is no such thing as difficult or easy—just different.

Puzzle 8

The female traveler comes to the riverbank with an ogre, a wolf, a goat, a head of cabbage, and a snake. The boat can carry three—the traveler herself and two others. As the traveler knows, if left alone together on either bank, without her, the ogre will eat the wolf, the wolf will eat the goat, and the goat will eat the cabbage. The ogre does not eat cabbage, goats, or snakes—just wolves. The wolf or goat does not eat snakes or ogres. And the snake does not eat any of the others. What is the least number of trips in total needed by the traveler to get them all across intact and continue with her journey?

Puzzle 9

The male traveler comes to the riverbank with an ogre, a wolf, a goat, a head of cabbage, and a snake. The boat is a strange one. It can hold the traveler with the goat and one other passenger (ogre, wolf, goat, cabbage, or snake), if needed; that is, three in total. Otherwise, it can hold only the traveler with one other (ogre, wolf, cabbage, or snake); that is, two in total. As before, if left alone on either bank, without the traveler, the ogre will eat the wolf, the wolf will eat the goat, and the goat will eat the cabbage. The ogre does not eat cabbage, goats or snakes. The wolf or goat will not eat snakes or ogres. And the snake does not eat any of the others. What is the least number of trips in total (not round trips) needed by the traveler to get them all across intact and continue with his journey?

Puzzle 10

The female traveler comes to the riverbank with a wolf, a goat, a cabbage, and a snake. The boat can carry only two—the traveler and one other. As before, if left alone together on either bank, without the traveler, the wolf will eat the goat and the goat will eat the cabbage. The wolf does not eat cabbage or snakes, and the goat does not eat snakes. The snake eats none of the others. What is the least number of trips in total (not round trips) needed by the traveler to get them all across intact and continue with her journey?

Alcuin composed a set of puzzles and collected them in a book to introduce young students to the importance of clear logical thinking. The book is titled *Propositiones ad acuendos juvenes* (*Problems to Sharpen the Young*). Some editions contain fifty-three puzzles, others fifty-six. It was translated into English by John Hadley and annotated by David Singmaster in 1992.

Finding a Way Across

Alcuin created several versions of his original puzzle. One of these involves groups of people. Let's do an easy one for the sake of illustration.

▸ ILLUSTRATION ◂

Two men and two women come to a riverbank wanting to go over to the other side. There is a boat there that can only carry two at one time. Here's the dilemma—a man and a woman cannot be left alone together on either side nor can a man and a woman alone together steer the boat across for some strange reason that need not concern us here. In any case, these are the conditions of the puzzle. How do the four get across given that any one of them can steer the boat?

Five trips in total are needed. Remember that a trip across or back is counted separately.

1. Let's start with the two men going across on the boat. We could have started with the two women, but the end result is the same.
2. When they get to the other side, one of them gets off and the other goes back alone. This is the second trip.
3. When he gets to the original side, the man gets off and the two women get on the boat and go across together. This is the third trip.
4. When they get to the other bank, the two women get off and the man who was there gets on and takes the trip back alone. This is the fourth trip taken.
5. When he gets there, he picks up the other man, taking the trip to the other bank together, where the two women are waiting to continue on with their journey.

▸ EASY ◂

To get started, try solving three similarly easy puzzles.

Puzzle 11

Two men and a woman come to a riverbank wanting to cross over to the other side. There is a boat there that can only carry two at one time. Here's the dilemma—either of the two men and the woman cannot be left alone together on either side or alone together on the boat. How many trips are required to get the three across under these conditions given that any one of them can steer the boat?

Puzzle 12

This time, one man and two women come to a riverbank wanting to cross over to the other side. Again, there is a boat that can only carry two at one time The man cannot be left alone with either one of the two women on either side or on the boat. How many trips are required to get the three across under these conditions given that any one of them can steer the boat?

Puzzle 13

This time, two men and two women come to a riverbank wanting to cross over to the other side. Again, there is a boat that can only carry two at one time. No man can be left alone with a woman unless there is another man or another woman present—on either side or on the boat. How many trips are required to get the four across under these conditions given that any one of them can steer the boat?

▸ MODERATELY HARD ◂

The dilemma is a little tougher to resolve in the next four puzzles.

Puzzle 14

One man, one woman, and a domestic cat come to a riverbank in order to cross over to the other side. There is a boat that can only carry two at one time. The cat cannot be left alone on either side or on the boat with the man, for some strange reason, without the presence of the woman. The cat can be left alone with the woman anywhere though, without the presence of the man. The man and woman can be together on either side or on the boat. Obviously, the cat cannot steer the boat. Also, the cat does not run away if left alone on either side. How many trips are required to cross over under these conditions given that either the man or the woman can steer the boat?

Puzzle 15

This time, two men, two women, and a domestic cat come to a riverbank in order to cross over to the other side. There is a boat that can only carry two at one time. The cat cannot be left alone on either side or on the boat with either man without the presence of at least one woman. The cat can be left alone with either of the two women anywhere though, without the presence of any man. The men and women can be left alone together in any combination on any side or on the boat. Of course, the cat cannot steer the boat. But the cat will not run away if left alone on either side. How many trips are required under these conditions given that any of the men or women can steer the boat?

Puzzle 16

A man, a woman, a domestic cat, and a domestic dog come to a riverbank in order to cross over to the other side. There is a boat that can only carry two at one time. Neither animal can be left alone on either side or on the boat with the man, without the presence of the woman. Either animal, or both, can be with the woman alone (without the man) anywhere. The man and woman can be alone on either side or on the boat. Of course, neither animal can steer the boat. How many trips are required to get to the other side under these conditions given that either the man or the woman can steer the boat?

Puzzle 17

This time, two men, one woman, and a domestic cat come to a riverbank in order to cross over to the other side. Again, there is a boat that can only carry two at one time. The cat cannot be left alone on either side or on the boat with either man, without the presence of the woman. The cat can be with the woman alone (without any man) anywhere. The two men and woman can be alone on either side or on the boat. Of course, the cat cannot steer the boat. How many trips are required to get to the other side under these conditions given that either the man or the woman can steer the boat?

▶ DIFFICULT ◀

Are you ready for some pretty complex river-crossing puzzles?

Puzzle 18

A man, a woman, one domestic cat, and two domestic dogs come to a riverbank in order to cross over to the other side. There is a boat that can carry two at one time. The cat cannot be left alone on either side or on the boat with the man alone, without the presence of the woman. The dogs can be with either the man or the woman alone anywhere. The man and woman can be alone on either side or on the boat. Of course, the animals cannot steer the boat. How many trips are required to get to the other side under these conditions given that either the man or the woman can steer the boat?

Puzzle 19

This time, a brother, a sister, and two domestic dogs come to a riverbank in order to cross over to the other side. Again, there is a boat that can only carry two at one time. The two dogs cannot be left alone together on either side, without the presence of the sister. Either one of the dogs can be left alone on either side, though. The brother cannot be left alone with either dog on either side (only the sister can). The brother can, however, transport either dog on the boat and the brother and sister can also go on the boat

126

together. Of course, neither dog can steer the boat. How many trips are required to get across to the other side under these conditions given that either the brother or the sister can steer the boat?

Puzzle 20

Two brothers, two sisters, and two domestic dogs come to a riverbank in order to cross over to the other side. Again, there is a boat that can only carry two at one time. Neither dog can be left alone on either side, without the presence of a sister. Either dog can be on the boat with either a brother or a sister. The two brothers, the two sisters, or a brother and sister pair can be together on the boat at any time. Of course, neither dog can steer the boat. How many trips are required to get across to the other side under these conditions given that either the brother or the sister can steer the boat?

More Dilemmas

The five puzzles in this final section give you more of the same, but this time they vary in difficulty, from easy to difficult. We will not tell you which is which.

Puzzle 21

A brother, a sister, a domestic cat, and a domestic dog come to a riverbank in order to cross over to the other side. The boat can carry only two at one time. The brother must be the last one going over to the other side and the cat the first. Of course, neither animal can steer the boat. How many trips are required to get to the other side under these conditions given that the brother or the sister can steer the boat?

River-crossing puzzles, involving different combinations of people, animals, and victuals, have been discovered across the world and across time. It is not certain if any of these predate Alcuin's puzzles.

Puzzle 22

A brother, a sister, their mother, and their father come to a riverbank wanting to cross over to the other side. There is a boat that can carry only two at one time. The mother must go over first. The second trip must be taken by the sister alone. The fourth trip must be taken by the brother alone. How many trips are required to get to the other side under these conditions given that anyone of the four can steer the boat?

Puzzle 23

A female traveler come to a riverbank with two wolves and three goats. The boat can carry no more than three—the traveler herself and two others. As you know, if left alone together on either bank, without the traveler, either of the wolves will eat any or all of the goats. What's the minimum number of trips required to transport all intact to the other side?

Puzzle 24

A traveler come to the riverbank with two ogres, two wolves, and two goats. There is a boat that can carry three at a time. As you know, if left alone together on either bank, either ogre will eat either or both wolves, and either wolf will eat either or both goats. Ogres do not eat goats and goats do not eat ogres. What is the least number of trips in total (not round trips) needed by the traveler to get everyone across safely and soundly and continue with the journey?

Puzzle 25

Here's one final conundrum. In the original puzzle—the traveler with a wolf, a goat, and a head of cabbage, and a boat with only two seats—could the trips be made safely without the possibility of going back to the original side with any one of the wolf, goat, and cabbage? That is, would the puzzle work if the traveler must go back to the original side always alone?

CHAPTER 8

Arrangement and Pairing Puzzles

Counting pairs is the oldest trick in combinatorics. . . .
Every time we count pairs, we learn something from it.
—GIL KALAI (B. 1955)

Arranging things and persons in a certain way, such as people around a table, is a common everyday event. Many kinds of puzzles have been devised based on arrangement, such as pairing off things and people in certain ways. This chapter is all about arrangements and pairings. These require a large dose of logic and common sense.

Seating Arrangements

Seating arrangements are a source of some truly interesting puzzles. The ten in this section involve seating arrangements. Let's do one together for the sake of illustration.

▶ ILLUSTRATION ◀

Four people, Alex (A), a man, Benny (B), another man, Carla (C), a woman, and Sarah (S), another woman, are seated at a table. Note that you must look down at the table diagram from above it.

1. Sarah's seat is shown in the diagram. The other three places are empty, as also shown.

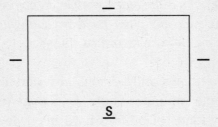

2. To her immediate left is a man.
3. Alex is seated right across from Sarah on the other side of the table.

   Complete the seating arrangement.

   First let's map out the clues. We are told that Alex is seated right across from Sarah. Let's put him there.

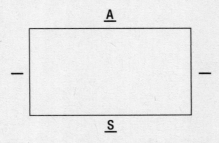

We are also told that a man is seated to Sarah's immediate left. The only other man is Benny. So let's put him to Sarah's immediate left.

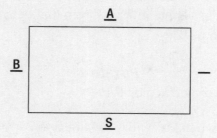

The remaining seat thus belongs to Carla.

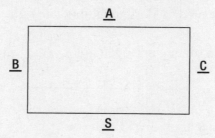

The formal study of how things can be arranged falls under the branch of mathematics known as combinatorial analysis, or combinatorics.

▸ EASY ◂

Remember that for all the puzzles in this section, you are looking down at a table from above it. So you must always visualize the orientations of the people involved from that perspective, just like in the illustration puzzle.

Puzzle 1

Four people are seated at a table.

- Bill (B), shown in his seat, is right next to Patty (P) on one of his sides.
- Directly in front of him, across the table, is Martha (M).
- Nick (N) is seated to Martha's immediate right.

Complete the seating arrangement.

Puzzle 2

Four people are seated at a table.

- There are two men, Sam (S) and Peter (P), and two women, Frieda (F) and Helen (H).
- The two men are not seated across from each other.
- Sam is seated as shown in the diagram.
- Directly across the table from Sam you will find Frieda.
- Seated to Frieda's immediate left is Helen.

Complete the seating arrangement.

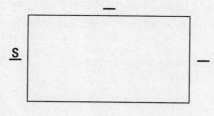

Puzzle 3

Four people are seated at a table.

- Jim (J), the only man, is seated as shown in the diagram.
- Deb (D) is seated to his immediate left.
- Katia (K) is seated to Deb's immediate left.
- The name of the third woman is Zelda (Z).

Complete the seating arrangement.

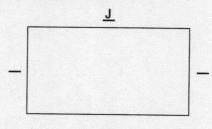

▸ MODERATELY HARD ◂

It is time to raise the difficulty notch a bit.

Puzzle 4

Five people are seated at a table.

- There are two men, Mark (M) and Pete (P). Pete is seated as shown in the diagram.
- There are three women, Caitlin (C), Lydia (L), and Samantha (S). One of them is seated to Peter's immediate left on his side of the table, where there are two seats available.
- Across the table from Pete and his female partner is Lydia.
- To Lydia's immediate left you will find Samantha.

Complete the seating arrangement.

Puzzles in arrangement, or combinatory logic, have provided mathematicians with key insights into properties of numbers and the nature of sets. This is perhaps why the great German philosopher, mathematician, and statesman Gottfried Leibniz (1646–1716) characterized logic as an *ars combinatoria*, a "combinatory art."

Puzzle 5

Six people are seated at a table. Note that on two of the sides there are two seats each.

- There are three men—Frank (F), Hank (H), and Jack (J)— and three women—Kelly (K), Laura (L), and Teresa (T). Frank is seated as shown in the diagram.
- On both sides where there are the two seats, you will find male and female pairs—that is, a man and a woman are seated next to each other on both these sides.
- Seated to Frank's immediate left is Jack.
- Directly across the table from Jack is Kelly.
- To Kelly's immediate right is Laura.

Complete the seating arrangement.

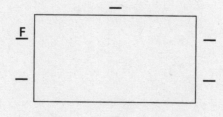

Puzzle 6

Eight people are seated at a table. Note that on each of the four sides there are two seats.

- There are four men—Andrew (A), Benny (B), Chris (C), Dan (D)—and four women—Emma (E), Irma (I), Lucy (L), Pina (P).
- Andrew is seated as shown. A woman is seated next to him on his side of the table.
- To his immediate right is Lucy. Her partner on her side is a man.
- Across the table, directly in front of Lucy, is Emma, who is seated right next to Benny on her side of the table.
- Pina is seated to Benny's immediate left.
- To Pina's immediate left on her side is Dan.

Complete the seating arrangement.

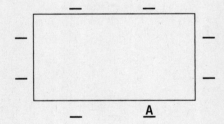

Puzzle 7

Eight people are seated at a table. On each of the four sides there are two seats.

- There are six women—Annie (A), Bertha (B), Chelsea (C), Glenda (G), Louise (L), Meagan (M)—and only two men—Rick (R) and Steve (S).
- Annie is seated as shown.
- The two men are seated together on one of the sides.
- To Annie's immediate right is Rick.
- Across the table from Rick, right in front of him, is Bertha.
- Chelsea is seated to Bertha's immediate right.
- Bertha is not paired with Louise or Meagan on her side of the table.
- Across the table from Chelsea, right in front of her, is Louise.

Complete the seating arrangement.

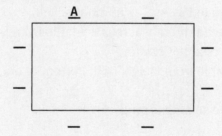

Today, combinatorics has important applications to the design and operation of computers, as well as to the physical sciences.

▸ DIFFICULT ◂

If you thought the previous puzzles were complex, try the next three!

Puzzle 8

Ten people are seated at a table. On two sides there are two seats each, as shown in the diagram. On the other two sides there are three seats each, also as shown in the diagram.

- There are five men—Arnie (A), Bob (B), Charlie (C), Dave (D), Ed (E)—and five women—Fanny (F), Georgia (G), Helga (H), Inez (I), Jasmine (J).
- Fanny is seated as shown in the diagram. Seated to her immediate left is Arnie.
- Three of the seats on the same side have only women in them.
- Across from Arnie on the other side of the table, right in front of him, is Inez. And seated right next to her is Georgia.
- Jasmine is seated to Arnie's immediate left.
- Fannie is seated directly across the table from Bob, who is seated right next to Charlie.
- Across the table from Helga, right in front of her, is Ed.

Complete the seating arrangement.

138

Puzzle 9

Ten people are seated at a table. On two sides there are two seats each, as shown in the diagram. On the other two sides there are three seats each, also as shown in the diagram.

- There are nine men—Al (A), Bart (B), Cam (C), Dick (D), Ernest (E), Harry (H), Kyle (K), Larry (L), Mick (M)—and one woman, Ruby (R), seated as shown in the diagram.
- The three men to her immediate right are Al, Bart, and Cam, but not necessarily in that order. Al is seated to Bart's left. And Cam is seated to Bart's right.
- Across the table from Bart, seated right in front of him, is Mick.
- To Mick's immediate right is Larry and to his immediate left is Kyle.
- To Kyle's left is Ernest.
- Directly across the table from Ernest, right in front of him, is Harry.

Complete the seating arrangement.

Puzzle 10

Ten people are seated at a table. The seats are shown in the diagram.

- There are five men—Cory (C), Don (D), Glen (G), Rory (R), Tim (T)—and five women—Amy (A), Bella (B), Ella (E), Judy (J), Katy (K).
- Amy is seated as shown. To her immediate left on the same side is a man. To his immediate left is Don. To Don's immediate left is Ella. She is seated directly across the table from Glen.
- Seated to Glen's immediate right is Judy. Directly across the table from Judy is Katy.
- To Katy's immediate left is Bella.
- Bella is seated directly across the table from Cory.
- Rory is seated on the same side as Glen.

Complete the seating arrangement.

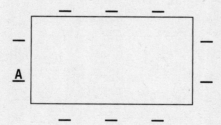

In any scientific area where the possible arrangements of a finite number of elements play a role, the logic used in combinatorial analysis is indispensable.

Pairing-Off Logic

Many things seem to come in pairs—two eyes, two ears, two feet, and so on. People also play cards in pairs, as well as some games, such as tennis or chess. Putting people into pairs in some specific way is a source of puzzles. The ten in this section are based on a "pairing-off logic." Let's do a very simple one for the sake of illustration.

▶ ILLUSTRATION ◀

Two men, Alex and Benny, and two women, Carla and Dina, want to go out together as two separate couples, made up of a man and a woman. Benny refuses to pair off with Dina. The others are fine with any pairing. Who make up the couples?

Benny—Carla
Alex—Dina

If Benny refuses to go with Dina, then he must go with Carla. This leaves Alex and Dina.

▶ EASY ◀

Here are three easy puzzles, just to get you started.

Puzzle 11

Three men, Andy, Bill, and Chuck, and three women, Emma, Nina, and Dina, want to go out together as couples, each couple made up of a man and a woman. Andy refuses to pair off with Dina and Dina refuses to pair off with Chuck. Chuck refuses to pair off with Emma. Everyone else is fine with any other pairing. What are the couples?

Puzzle 12

Six women—Andrea, Bea, Lara, Mary, Noreen, Rita—want to play cards in separate pairs. Andrea, Bea, Rita, and Mary refuse to play with Noreen. Bea and Rita refuse to play with each other. And Bea refuses to play with Andrea. What are the pairings?

Puzzle 13

Six men this time—Alex, Billy, Lucky, Manny, Nicky, Ron—want to play cards in separate pairs. Alex is paired with Lucky. Manny refuses to play with Nicky or Ron. What are the pairings?

▶ MODERATELY HARD ◀

The next four puzzles will challenge your skills at combinatory logic a bit more.

Puzzle 14

Five men—Art, Charles, Gus, Jack, Pat—all want to go on a date with Helen. But Helen has her mind made up to go out with one in particular. Here's the relevant information.

1. Art, Charles, and Gus are good friends. So too are Jack and Pat. The two sets of friends do no know each other—that is, Art, Charles, and Gus do no know Jack and Pat (and vice versa, of course).
2. Helen refuses to go out with Gus or any of his friends.
3. She has already gone out with Jack, and so wants to date someone different, and she does so.

Who does Helen end up dating?

Puzzle 15

Five people—Amy, Charlotte, Guy, Jasmine, Pina—all want to play a game of tennis with Trina.

1. Trina does not want to play with anyone with whom she has already played, including Pina.
2. She also refuses to play with anyone who has beaten her sister, Amy, including Guy. Needless to say, she has played with Amy many times and so does not want to play with her again.
3. Trina has played several times with Jasmine.

Given these facts, who should Trina play with?

Puzzle 16

The following six students are paired with each other for an upcoming race competition: three girls (Claudia, Delia, and Paula) and three boys (Alex, Mark, and Len).

1. The three pairs are to be made up of a boy and girl each.
2. Claudia is not paired with either Mark or Len.
3. Mark is not paired with Delia.

What are the pairs?

Puzzle 17

The following eight students are to be paired with each other for an upcoming chess competition: Andrew, Becky, Crandall, Dora, Ella, Greta, Ivan, Pavi.

1. Each pair is to be made up of two people who have never played against each other previously.
2. Andrew has played against Dora, Greta, and Pavi.
3. Ivan has played against Ella, Crandall, and Andrew.
4. Ella and Crandall have also played against Andrew.
5. Dora and Greta have played against Ivan.
6. Greta has also played against Crandall and Dora.

What are the pairs?

▶ DIFFICULT ◀

The next three puzzles are quite intricate. Good luck!

Puzzle 18

A scorecard lists the following pairs of card players who played against each other yesterday.

Art—Zina
Bill—Yolanda
Greg—Ken
Lucia—Mark

As it turns out, these are all wrong. Art did not play against Zina, Bill against Yolanda, Greg against Ken, and Lucia against Mark. We can tell you that:

1. Lucia did not play against Bill, Art, or Greg.
2. Neither did Ken or Zina play against Lucia.
3. Art did not play against Bill, Greg, or Ken.
4. Bill did not play against Ken or Zina.

What were the correct pairings?

Puzzle 19

Ten people—five men (Andy, Barney, Charlie, Dave, Ed) and five women (Fiona, Gaia, Hillary, Irma, Jill)—played against each other in a chess tournament yesterday, two per match.

1. One match had Andy play against a woman. Another match had Barney also play against a woman, but not Irma.
2. Charlie played against Dave and Ed against Fiona.
3. Hillary and Gaia were paired off against each other.

What were the correct pairings of players?

Puzzle 20

Three men, Andrew, Bob, and Chuck, and three women, Ella, Nora, and Debbie, want to go out together as couples, each couple made up of a man and a woman. Here are a few facts that you should know.

1. Andrew is older than Bob, and Bob is older than Chuck.
2. Ella refuses to go out with anyone younger than Bob. So too does Nora.
3. Ella is taller than Nora, but shorter than Debbie.
4. Bob refuses to go out with the shortest of the women.

What are the couples?

Seating Arrangements, Again!

For the last five puzzles in this chapter let's get back to seating arrangements. In this case the five puzzles are all connected, as you will soon discover. You have to solve the puzzles in order and keep each solution handy. Good luck!

Puzzle 21

Four people are to be seated at a table—Calvin (C), Mick (M), Ornella (O), and Wynn (W).

- Calvin is seated as shown.
- Wynn does not sit across the table from Calvin.
- Mick sits to the immediate left of Wynn.

Complete the seating arrangement.

Puzzle 22

After having completed the previous puzzle, you must use your solution for this one. Jane (J) and Randy (R) are to be seated at the same table as Calvin (C), Mick (M), Ornella (O), and Wynn (W). The last four remain in their places according to Puzzle 21, maybe just moving seats slightly to accommodate the new guests. Here's how Jane and Ruby are to be added to the seating.

- Two extra seats are added, as shown in the diagram.
- Randy is seated right next to Wynn.
- Jane is seated right next to Ornella.

Complete the seating arrangement.

Puzzle 23

For this puzzle you have to carry over the solution of the previous one (Puzzle 22). Alex (A) and Sarah (S) have to be added to the seating arrangement along with Jane (J), Randy (R), Calvin (C), Mick (M), Ornella (O), and Wynn (W)—all of whom have their seats according to the solution of the previous puzzle.

- Two more seats are added as shown in the diagram.
- Alex is seated to Mick's immediate right and directly across from Sarah.

Complete the seating arrangement.

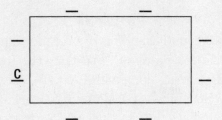

Puzzle 24

For this puzzle you have to carry over the solution to the previous one (Puzzle 23). Brett (B) is now added to the table along with Alex (A), Sarah (S), Jane (J), Randy (R), Calvin (C), Mick (M), Ornella (O), and Wynn (W)—all of whom have their seats according to the solution of the previous puzzle.

- The new seat is added to the diagram below.
- Simply put Brett in it. Note he will be sitting to Jane's immediate right.

Complete the seating arrangement.

Puzzle 25

For this last puzzle you have to carry over the solution for the previous one (Puzzle 24). Frank (F) and Lucy (L) are now added to the seating arrangement along with Brett (B), Alex (A), Sarah (S), Jane (J), Randy (R), Calvin (C), Mick (M), Ornella (O), and Wynn (W)—all of whom have their seats according to the solution of the previous puzzle.

- The two new seats are shown in the diagram.
- Frank is seated to the immediate left of Randy.
- Lucy is seated to the immediate right of Brett.

Complete the final seating arrangement.

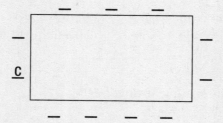

Throughout this book you have hopefully experienced how intriguing logic puzzles are. I would like to suggest that logical thinking is a skill that can be cultivated, especially with puzzles!

Answers

Chapter 1

Puzzle 1: 12

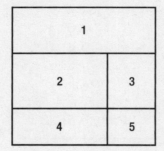

STAND-ALONES	ASSEMBLED
1. 1	6. 1+2+3
2. 2	7. 1+2+3+4+5 (the overall
3. 3	containing square)
4. 4	8. 2+3
5. 5	9. 2+3+4+5
	10. 2+4
	11. 3+5
	12. 4+5

From now on, the list of figures will include both stand-alones and assembled figures. There is no need to separate them out any longer since you know what is going on, right? If you wish, you can continue on your own to separate the two.

Puzzle 2: 10

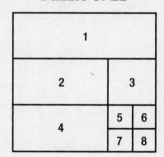

1. 1
2. 1+2+3+4+5
3. 2
4. 2+3
5. 2+3+4

6. 2+3+4+5
7. 3
8. 4
9. 4+5
10. 5

Puzzle 3: 22

1. 1
2. 1+2+3
3. 1+2+3+4+5+6+7+8
4. 2
5. 2+3
6. 2+3+4+5+6+7+8
7. 2+4
8. 3
9. 3+5+6
10. 3+5+6+7+8
11. 4

12. 4+5+7
13. 4+5+6+7+8
14. 5
15. 5+6
16. 5+6+7+8
17. 5+7
18. 6
19. 6+8
20. 7
21. 7+8
22. 8

Puzzle 4: 9

Note: not all numbered segments are triangles in themselves, but may be part of assembled ones.

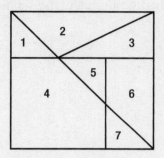

Note, first, that the segments numbered 4 and 6 are not triangles in themselves but are part of assembled triangles.

1. 1
2. 2
3. 3
4. 5
5. 7
6. 1+4+7
7. 2+3+5+6
8. 3+5+6
9. 5+6

Puzzle 5: 13

Note: not all numbered segments are triangles in themselves, but may be part of assembled ones.

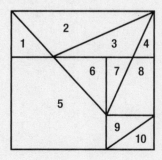

Note, first, that the segment numbered 8 is not a triangle in itself but is part of an assembled triangle. Also note that the segment numbered 5 does not play any role in assemblage— it just completes the numbering of the segments.

1. 1
2. 2
3. 2+3+6+7
4. 3
5. 3+4
6. 3+6+7
7. 4

8. 4+8
9. 6
10. 6+7
11. 7
12. 9
13. 10

Puzzle 6: 16

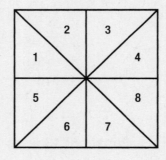

1. 1
2. 1+2+3+5
3. 1+5
4. 1+5+6+7
5. 2
6. 2+3
7. 2+3+4+8
8. 3

9. 4
10. 4+6+7+8
11. 4+8
12. 5
13. 6
14. 6+7
15. 7
16. 8

Puzzle 7: 25

Note: not all numbered segments are triangles in themselves, but may be part of assembled ones.

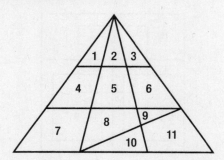

Note, first, that the segments numbered 4, 5, 6, 7, 8, and 11 are not triangles in themselves but are part of assembled triangles.

1. 1
2. 1+2
3. 1+2+3
4. 1+2+3+4+5+6
5. 1+2+3+4+5+6+7+8+9+10+11
6. 1+2+4+5
7. 1+2+4+5+7+8+10
8. 1+4
9. 1+4+7
10. 2
11. 2+3
12. 2+3+5+6
13. 2+3+5+6+8+9
14. 2+3+5+6+8+9+10+11
15. 2+5
16. 2+5+8
17. 2+5+8+10
18. 3
19. 3+6
20. 3+6+9
21. 3+6+9+11
22. 8+9
23. 9
24. 10
25. 10+11

Puzzle 8: 14

Note: not all numbered segments are squares or rectangles in themselves, but may be part of assembled ones.

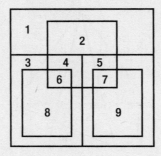

Note, first, that the segments numbered 1, 3, 4, 5, 8, and 9 are not squares or rectangles in themselves but are part of assembled squares or rectangles.

1. 1+2
2. 1+2+3+4+5+6+7+8+9
3. 2
4. 2+4+5+6+7
5. 3+4+5+6+7+8+9
6. 3+4+6+8
7. 4+5+6+7
8. 4+6
9. 5+7
10. 5+7+9
11. 6
12. 6+8
13. 7
14. 7+9

Puzzle 9: 36

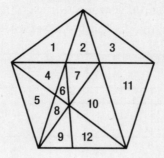

1. 1
2. 1+2
3. 1+2+3
4. 1+2+4+6+7+10
5. 1+4
6. 1+4+5
7. 2
8. 2+3
9. 2+6+7+8
10. 2+6+7+10
11. 2+6+7+8+9+10+12
12. 3
13. 3+11
14. 4
15. 4+5
16. 4+5+6+7+8
17. 4+6
18. 4+6+7

19. 4+6+7+10
20. 4+6+7+10+11
21. 5
22. 5+8
23. 5+8+9+12
24. 6
25. 6+7+8
26. 6+8
27. 6+8+9
28. 7
29. 8
30. 8+9+12
31. 9
32. 9+10+12
33. 9+12
34. 10
35. 11
36. 12

Puzzle 10: 27

Note: not all numbered segments are squares or rectangles in themselves, but may be part of assembled ones.

Note, first, that the segments numbered 1, 4, 5, and 6 are not squares or rectangles in themselves but are part of assembled squares or rectangles.

1. 1+2
2. 1+2+3+4+5+7+8+9+10
3. 1+2+3+5+7+8+9
4. 1+2+7+8
5. 2
6. 2+5+8+9
7. 2+5+8+9+10
8. 2+5+8+9+10+11+12
9. 2+8
10. 3
11. 3+4+5+9+10
12. 3+5+9
13. 4+10
14. 5+9
15. 5+9+10
16. 6+7+8+9+11
17. 7
18. 7+8
19. 7+8+9
20. 8
21. 8+9
22. 8+9+11
23. 9
24. 10
25. 11
26. 11+12
27. 12

Puzzle 11: 5 triangles

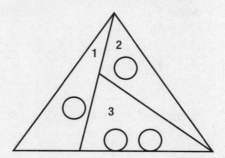

1. Triangle 1: one circle
2. Triangle 2: one circle
3. Triangle 3: two circles
4. Triangle 1+2+3: four circles
5. Triangle 2+3: three circles

Puzzle 12: 6 triangles

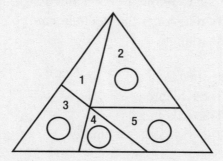

Note that not all the numbered triangles contain circles. Triangle 1 is empty. Also note that not all numbered segments are triangles in themselves, but they may be part of assembled ones. The segments numbered 3 and 5 are not triangles. Always remember that a circle can be contained by more than one triangle.

1. Triangle 1+2+3+4+5: four circles
2. Triangle 1+3: one circle
3. Triangle 2: one circle
4. Triangle 2+4+5: three circles
5. Triangle 3+4: two circles
6. Triangle 4: one circle

Puzzle 13: 11 triangles

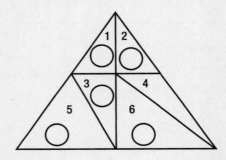

Not all numbered triangles contain circles. Triangle 4 is empty. Always remember that a circle can be contained by more than one triangle.

1. Triangle 1: one circle
2. Triangle 1+2: two circles
3. Triangle 1+3: two circles
4. Triangle 1+2+3+4+5+6: five circles
5. Triangle 1+3+5: three circles
6. Triangle 2: one circle
7. Triangle 2+4: one circle (Did you miss this one?)
8. Triangle 2+4+6: two circles
9. Triangle 3: one circle
10. Triangle 5: one circle
11. Triangle 6: one circle

Puzzle 14: 17 triangles

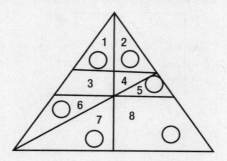

Triangle 4 is empty. Segments 3 and 8 are not triangles in themselves, but are part of assembled ones. Always remember that a circle can be contained by more than one triangle.

1. Triangle 1: one circle
2. Triangle 1+2: two circles
3. Triangle 1+2+3+4+5: three circles
4. Triangle 1+2+3+4+6: three circles
5. Triangle 1+2+3+4+5+6+7+8: six circles
6. Triangle 1+3: one circle
7. Triangle 1+3+6: two circles
8. Triangle 1+3+6+7: three circles
9. Triangle 2: one circle
10. Triangle 2+4: one circle
11. Triangle 2+4+5: two circles
12. Triangle 2+4+5+8: three circles
13. Triangle 3+4+6: one circle
14. Triangle 5: one circle
15. Triangle 5+7+8: three circles
16. Triangle 6: one circle
17. Triangle 7: one circle

Puzzle 15: 11 triangles

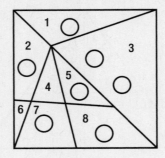

Triangles 4 and 6 are empty. Segments 7 and 8 are not triangles in themselves, but are part of assembled ones. Always remember that a circle can be contained by more than one triangle.

1. Triangle 1: one circle
2. Triangle 1+3: three circles
3. Triangle 2+4+5: two circles
4. Triangle 2+4+5+6+7+8: four circles
5. Triangle 2+6: one circle
6. Triangle 3: two circles
7. Triangle 4+5: one circle
8. Triangle 4+5+7+8: three circles
9. Triangle 4+7: one circle
10. Triangle 5: one circle
11. Triangle 5+8: two circles

Puzzle 16: 13 triangles

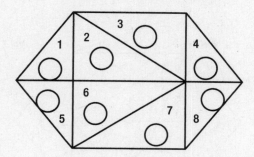

Always remember that a circle can be contained by more than one triangle.

1. Triangle 1: one circle
2. Triangle 1+2: two circles
3. Triangle 1+5: two circles
4. Triangle 2: one circle
5. Triangle 2+6: two circles
6. Triangle 3: one circle
7. Triangle 4: one circle
8. Triangle 4+8: two circles
9. Triangle 5: one circle
10. Triangle 5+6: two circles
11. Triangle 6: one circle
12. Triangle 7: one circle
13. Triangle 8: one circle

Puzzle 17: 10 triangles

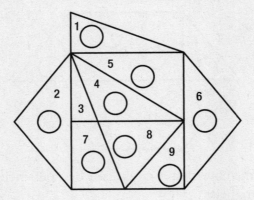

Triangle 3 is empty. Segment 7 is not a triangle in itself but is part of an assembled one. Always remember that a circle can be contained by more than one triangle.

1. Triangle 1: one circle
2. Triangle 2: one circle
3. Triangle 3+4: one circle
4. Triangle 3+7: one circle
5. Triangle 4: one circle
6. Triangle 4+8: two circles
7. Triangle 5: one circle
8. Triangle 6: one circle
9. Triangle 8: one circle
10. Triangle 9: one circle

Puzzle 18: 16 triangles

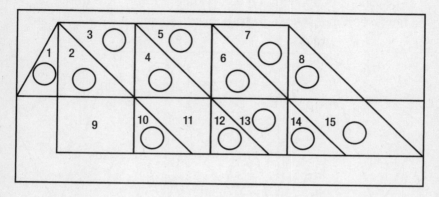

Segments 9, 11, 13, and 15 are not triangles in themselves but may be part of assembled ones. Always remember that a circle can be contained by more than one triangle.

1. Triangle 1: one circle
2. Triangle 1+2: two circles
3. Triangle 2: one circle
4. Triangle 2+9+10: two circles
5. Triangle 3: one circle
6. Triangle 4: one circle
7. Triangle 4+10+11+12: three circles
8. Triangle 5: one circle
9. Triangle 6: one circle
10. Triangle 6+12+13+14: four circles
11. Triangle 7: one circle
12. Triangle 8: one circle
13. Triangle 8+14+15: three circles
14. Triangle 10: one circle
15. Triangle 12: one circle
16. Triangle 14: one circle

Puzzle 19: 10 triangles

This one is actually much easier than it looks. It is in the difficult section just to keep you on your toes.

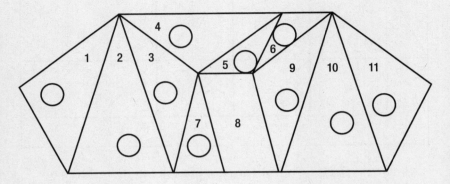

Segment 8 is not a triangle—it has been numbered simply for completeness.

1. Triangle 1: one circle
2. Triangle 2: one circle
3. Triangle 3: one circle
4. Triangle 4: one circle
5. Triangle 5: one circle
6. Triangle 6: one circle
7. Triangle 7: one circle
8. Triangle 9: one circle
9. Triangle 10: one circle
10. Triangle 11: one circle

Puzzle 20: 35 triangles

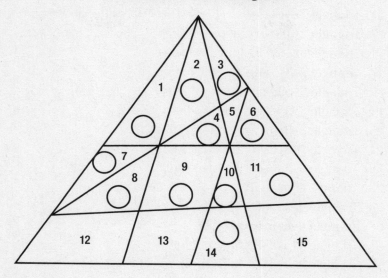

Triangle 5 is empty. Segments 9, 11, 12, 13, 14, and 15 are not triangles in themselves but may be part of assembled ones. Always remember that a circle can be contained by more than one triangle.

1. Triangle 1: one circle
2. Triangle 1+2+3+4+5+6: five circles
3. Triangle 1+2+3+4+5+6+7+8+9+10+11: ten circles
4. Triangle 1+2+3+4+5+6+7+8+9+10+11+12+13+14+15: eleven circles
5. Triangle 1+2+4: three circles
6. Triangle 1+2+4+7+8+9+10: seven circles
7. Triangle 1+2+4+7+8+9+10+12+13+14: eight circles
8. Triangle 1+2+7: three circles
9. Triangle 1+2+3+7: four circles
10. Triangle 2: one circle
11. Triangle 2+3: two circles
12. Triangle 2+3+4+5+6: four circles

13. Triangle 2+3+4+5+6+9+10+11: seven circles
14. Triangle 2+3+4+5+6+9+10+11+13+14+15: eight circles
15. Triangle 2+4: two circles
16. Triangle 2+4+9+10: four circles
17. Triangle 2+4+9+10+13+14: five circles
18. Triangle 3: one circle
19. Triangle 3+5: one circle
20. Triangle 3+5+6: two circles
21. Triangle 3+5+6+11: three circles
22. Triangle 3+5+6+11+15: three circles
23. Triangle 4: one circle
24. Triangle 4+5: one circle
25. Triangle 4+5+6: two circles
26. Triangle 4+5+8+9: three circles
27. Triangle 4+5+6+8+9+10+11: six circles
28. Triangle 4+8+9+10: four circles
29. Triangle 6: one circle
30. Triangle 6+10+11: three circles
31. Triangle 6+10+11+14+15: four circles
32. Triangle 7: one circle
33. Triangle 8: one circle
34. Triangle 10: one circle
35. Triangle 10+14: two circles

Puzzle 21: 30

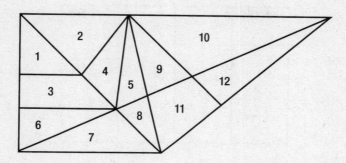

Segments 3 and 11 are not triangles in themselves, but are part of assembled ones.

1. 1
2. 1+2+3+4+5+6+9+10
3. 1+3
4. 1+3+6
5. 1+3+6+7
6. 2
7. 2+4
8. 2+4+5+8
9. 2+4+5+9+10
10. 4
11. 4+5
12. 4+5+8
13. 5
14. 5+8
15. 5+9

16. 5+9+10
17. 6
18. 7
19. 7+8
20. 7+8+11+12
21. 8
22. 8+11+12
23. 9
24. 9+10
25. 9+10+11+12
26. 9+11
27. 10
28. 10+12
29. 11+12
30. 12

Puzzle 22: 18

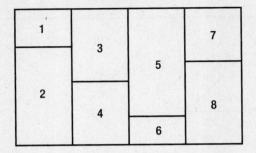

Always remember that there are stand-alone and assembled figures.

1. 1
2. 1+2
3. 1+2+3+4
4. 1+2+3+4+5+6
5. 1+2+3+4+5+6+7+8
6. 2
7. 3
8. 3+4
9. 3+4+5+6
10. 3+4+5+6+7+8
11. 4
12. 5
13. 5+6
14. 5+6+7+8
15. 6
16. 7
17. 7+8
18. 8

Puzzle 23: 16

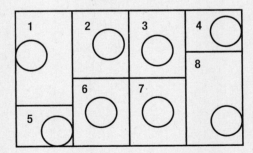

Figure = square or rectangle

1. Figure 1: one circle
2. Figure 1+5: two circles

3. Figure 1+2+5+6: four circles
4. Figure 1+2+3+5+6+7: six circles
5. Figure 1+2+3+4+5+6+7+8: eight circles
6. Figure 2: one circle
7. Figure 2+6: two circles
8. Figure 2+3: two circles
9. Figure 2+3+6+7: four circles
10. Figure 2+3+4+6+7+8: six circles
11. Figure 3: one circle
12. Figure 3+7: two circles
13. Figure 3+4+7+8: four circles
14. Figure 4: one circle
15. Figure 4+8: two circles
16. Figure 8: one circle

Puzzle 24: 29

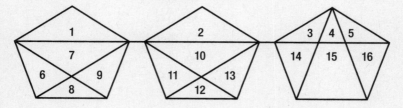

Always remember that there are stand-alone and assembled triangles.

1. 1	11. 5+16	21. 10+11
2. 2	12. 6	22. 10+13
3. 3	13. 6+7	23. 11
4. 3+4	14. 6+8	24. 11+12
5. 3+4+5	15. 7	25. 12
6. 3+14	16. 7+9	26. 12+13
7. 4	17. 8	27. 13
8. 4+5	18. 8+9	28. 14
9. 4+15	19. 9	29. 16
10. 5	20. 10	

Puzzle 25: 18

```
┌─────┬─────────────────────────┐
│  1  │  2                      │
│     │       ┌─────────────┐   │
│     │       │  3          │   │
├─────┼─────┬─┴───────────┬─┤   │
│     │     │             │ │   │
│  4  │  5  │  6          │ │ 7 │
│     │     │             │ │   │
└─────┴─────┴─────────────┴─┴───┘
```

Always remember that there are stand-alone and assembled squares and rectangles.

1. 1	10. 4+5
2. 1+2+3	11. 4+5+6
3. 1+2+3+4+5+6+7	12. 4+5+6+7
4. 1+4	13. 5
5. 2+3	14. 5+6
6. 2+3+5+6+7	15. 5+6+7
7. 3	16. 6
8. 3+6	17. 6+7
9. 4	18. 7

Chapter 2

Puzzle 1

Puzzle 2

Puzzle 3

Puzzle 4

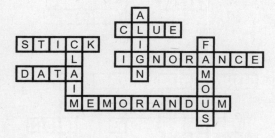

Puzzle 5

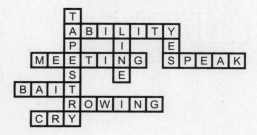

Puzzle 6

Puzzle 7

Puzzle 8

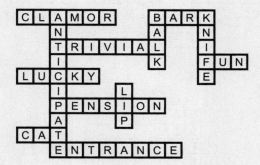

Puzzle 9

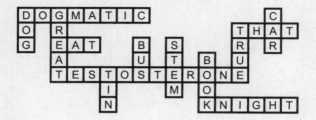

Puzzle 10

Puzzle 11

1. HATE
2. TEN
3. MUCH
4. SNOW

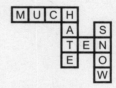

Puzzle 12

1. STOP
2. TRY
3. HELLO
4. LEAVE

Puzzle 13

1. LITTLE
2. TIGHT
3. GLUE
4. UP
5. LET

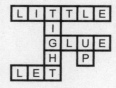

Puzzle 14

1. BELOW
2. BEHIND
3. CHART
4. RUN
5. NEVER
6. FRIEND

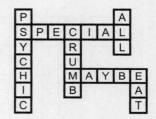

Puzzle 15

1. PSYCHIC
2. SPECIAL
3. CRUMB
4. MAYBE
5. ALL
6. EAT

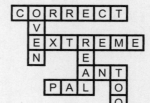

Puzzle 16

1. CORRECT
2. OVEN
3. EXTREME
4. REAL
5. ANT
6. PAL
7. TOO

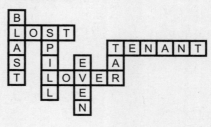

Puzzle 17

1. BLAST
2. LOST
3. SPILL
4. LOVER
5. EVEN
6. TAR
7. TENANT

Puzzle 18

1. VENDOR
2. NOBLE
3. ABILITY
4. TABLE
5. BASKET
6. KIT
7. SPIT
8. PICK

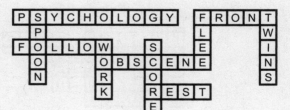

Puzzle 19

1. ALLOW
2. LENIENT
3. NEST
4. TOGETHER
5. GET
6. CHIN
7. ROAR
8. OPEN
9. NIL

Puzzle 20

1. PSYCHOLOGY
2. SPOON
3. FOLLOW
4. WORK
5. OBSCENE
6. SCORE
7. REST
8. FLEE
9. FRONT
10. TWINS

Puzzle 21

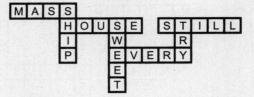

Puzzle 22

Puzzle 23

Puzzle 24

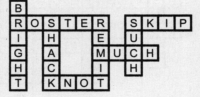

Puzzle 25

Chapter 3

Puzzle 1

A: 2 blue
B: 1 red
C: 2 red

Since someone drew a blue ball from Box A, we can now be sure that it contains the two blue balls. There are now only red balls left (one red or two red). B's label says it contains two red, but this is false. So it contains one red ball, and this leaves the two red for C.

Puzzle 2

A: 3 blue
B: 3 green
C: 1 red, 1 blue, 1 green

Since Box A is labeled incorrectly, we know it does not contain one red, one blue, and one green. So it contains either three blue balls or three green balls. Since a blue ball was drawn from A, it means that it contains three blue ones. We know that Box C does not contain three green balls, because of the wrong label, and it does not contain three blue balls (A does). So by elimination, it contains one red, one blue, and one green ball. This means that Box B contains the remaining three green balls.

Puzzle 3

A: 1 red
B: 5 red, 5 blue, 5 green
C: zero balls

If someone draws a green ball from any box, it means that it will contain the five red, five blue, and five green balls, since the other two boxes do not contain any green balls. Since a green ball was drawn from Box B, it means that it is the one with the five red, five blue, and five green balls. We know that Box C does not contain the one red ball because of the mislabeling, and it's not the box with the five red, five blue, and five green balls (B is). So it contains zero balls. This means that Box A contains the remaining red ball.

Puzzle 4

A: 2 green, 1 red
B: 5 red
C: 1 blue

Drawing more than one red ball from any box means that it will contain the five red balls, since there is only a single red ball in one of the other boxes. This means that the five red balls are in B, from which three red balls were drawn. Box C does not contain the two green balls and one red ball, because it is mislabeled. So it contains one blue ball, and by elimination A contains two green balls and one red ball.

Puzzle 5

A: 1 red, 1 white
B: 1 green, 1 white
C: 9 red, 1 white

As in the previous puzzle, drawing more than one red ball from any box means that it will contain the nine red balls, since there is only a single red ball in one of the other boxes. This means that the set of nine red balls and the one white one is in C, from which two red balls were drawn. B's label says that it contains one red and one white, but this is wrong because of the incorrect label; and it does not contain the nine red and one white (C does). So it contains one green and one white. This leaves one red and one white in A.

Puzzle 6

A: 2 red, 3 white
B: 2 green
C: 2 white, 1 red

Consider Box B. It has just two balls within it. Since the only color of the balls is green (as indicated), we can conclude that the color of both balls is green. The red and white balls are distributed in Boxes A and C, adding up to eight balls in total as can be seen from the top labels. We are told that there are three white balls in one of the boxes. That box cannot be C, because it has three in total and at least one of these has to be red. So Box A is the one with three white balls, meaning that its two remaining balls are red. The other two white balls are in C, which has three balls in total, meaning that it has one red ball.

Puzzle 7

A: 1 blue, 1 red, 2 green, 1 white
B: 1 blue, 2 red
C: 1 blue, 2 white

There are three blue balls in total, and so we can easily see from the color contents of the three boxes that each one has a single blue ball in it. Consider Box B. It has three balls in it, colored blue and red. We have just discovered that it has one blue ball. So the other two balls must be red. We are told that there are three red balls in total. So the other one is in Box A. Now consider Box C. We know it has one blue ball inside. We can now deduce that the other two are colored white.

Now consider Box A. It has four colors in it. We have discovered that there is one blue and one red in it. We are told that there are three white balls overall, and two of them are in C. So the remaining white ball is in A. We have now figured out that there are one blue, one red, and one white ball in A. The remaining two balls are, therefore, green ones—remember that A has five balls in total.

Puzzle 8

A: 4 blue, 1 red
B: 1 blue, 4 green
C: 1 red, 9 white

We are told that there are two red balls in total. One of them is in Box A and the other is in Box C—as can be deduced from the color labels. Now consider Box C. It has two colors in it and ten balls. One of these, as we have just discovered, is red. So the remaining nine are white. In Box A, of the five balls, we have discovered that one is red. The other color in the box is blue. So the remaining four balls are blue. There are five blue balls in total, so the remaining one is in B, meaning that the other four balls in it are green.

Puzzle 9

A: 3 blue, 6 green
B: 1 blue, 5 red, 1 green
C: 1 white, 1 blue

Let's start with an easy deduction. Box C has two balls in it, and the label says that it has two colors. So one is white and one is blue.

We are told that there are five red balls in total, and they are all in Box B, as can be deduced by its color label (the only box with red balls in it). There are seven balls in total, so the remaining two balls are one blue and one green.

We are told that there are seven green balls in total. We found that one is in B. So the other six are in A. Since A has nine total balls in it, the remaining three are blue.

Puzzle 10

A: 4 red, 1 white
B: 2 blue, 3 green
C: 3 blue, 1 white

Only Box A has red balls in it, and since we are told that there are four in total, it has the four red balls plus one white ball (five balls in total). We are also told that there are two white balls in total. One is in A, as we have discovered, so the other must be in C. The remaining three balls in C are, therefore, blue ones. There are five blue balls in total, so the other two blue balls are in B. From the top label, this means that the number of green balls in it is three.

Puzzle 11: B

Since all the labels are true, it is easy to follow their implications.

A: "The coin is not in here"—true, so it is in B or C
B: "The coin is not in C"—true, so it is not in C

This leaves B as the only possibility, since we have eliminated A and C. C's label is true, clearly, but it changes nothing.

Puzzle 12: C

All three labels are false. So A's label claiming that the coin is within it eliminates A (since it is false). Similarly, B's label claiming that the coin is within it eliminates B (since it is also false). This means that C is the container of the coin. C's label—"The coin is in B"—is false, but changes nothing.

Puzzle 13: B

The label on B and the label on C contradict each other. So one is true and the other is false. At this point we cannot be sure which is which. But we have located where the false label is—on B or C, but not therefore on A, of course. This means that A's label is the other true one. It says that the coin is in B. And that's where it is. Now we can see that B's label is clearly false while C's is true.

Puzzle 14: C

The labels on A and B contradict each other. So one is true and the other is false. At this point we cannot be sure which is which. But we have located where the single true label is—on A or B, but not therefore on C, of course. We can now deduce that the label on C is a false statement. It says that the coin is not within the box. But we have just concluded that this is false. So, contrary to what it says, the coin is in C. We can now see that A's label is true while B's is false. Nothing changes, though.

Puzzle 15: C

Labels A and C say the same thing—namely, that the coin is in B. So they are either both true or both false. If they are both true, then the coin is actually in B, making B's label true as well—if the coin is in B, then it cannot be in A (as the label says). But we are told that there is at least one false label, not three true ones. So we reject the hypothesis that A and C are true, since it leads to an inconsistency. Therefore, they are both false, making label B true. From all this, we deduce that the coin is not in B, contrary to what A and C say, and it is not in A, as the label on B truthfully asserts. So it is in C.

Puzzle 16: B

We are told that the coin is not in C, and since labels A and C are consistent with that statement, those labels are true. This means that the label on B is false because there is one false label. We are told that the box with a false label on it is also the one with the coin in it, and there is only one of those boxes—B.

Puzzle 17: A

The labels on A and C say the same thing—namely, that the coin is not in B. So they are either both true or both false. They cannot be false since we are told that there is only one false label among the three. So they are both true. This means two things: (a) the coin is not in B as the labels indicate, and (b) B's label is the false one. So, contrary to what it says, the coin is also not in C. By process of elimination, the coin is in A.

Puzzle 18: C

Labels A and B say the same thing—namely, that the coin is not in B. So they are either both true or both false. They cannot be false since there was only one false label. So, they are both true. The false label is therefore on C. We are told that the box with the false label contains the coin, so it must be in C. We can now confirm that what C's label states is indeed false.

Puzzle 19: B

The labels on A and C say the same thing—namely, that the coin is in A. So they are either both true or both false. They cannot both be true, since we are told that there is only one true label among the three. So they are both false. This means that B's label is the only true one and, therefore, that Box B contains the coin.

Puzzle 20: C

This is an easy one. Did you miss it? This was put in the difficult section on purpose to keep you on your logical toes. A and B say the same thing—namely, that the coin is not in A. So they are either both true or both false. They cannot both be false, since there is only one false label. So they are both true. This means C's label is false, and, contrary to what C's label says, the coin is indeed in C.

Puzzle 21

Given the nine weights, the fact that each box should contain the same total weight, and the three weights already inserted, the only possibility for equal weight distribution (15 lbs. per box) is as follows.

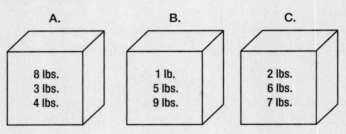

A.
8 lbs.
3 lbs.
4 lbs.

B.
1 lb.
5 lbs.
9 lbs.

C.
2 lbs.
6 lbs.
7 lbs.

Puzzle 22

This puzzle requires some trial and error, but in the end you will find that the box weights that work are: A = 20 lbs.; B = 10 lbs.; C = 10 lbs. So the other weights have to be distributed as shown. There is no other way to make the equation A = B + C hold. So, the contents of the boxes are as follows.

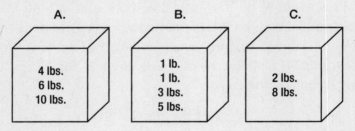

A.
4 lbs.
6 lbs.
10 lbs.

B.
1 lb.
1 lb.
3 lbs.
5 lbs.

C.
2 lbs.
8 lbs.

Puzzle 23

This puzzle also requires some trial and error, but in the end you will find that the box weights that work are: A = 4 lbs.; B = 7 lbs.; C = 11 lbs. So the other weights have to be distributed as shown. There is no other way to make the equation A + B = C hold. So, the contents of the boxes are as follows.

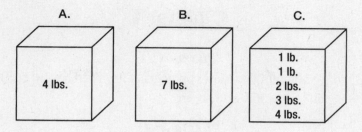

Puzzle 24

The constant weight is 14 lbs. per box. The weights are distributed as follows according to the number on each top label. There is no other way to distribute the weights.

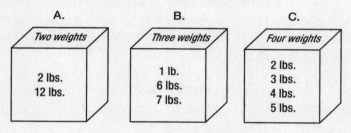

Puzzle 25

Like the previous puzzles, there is some trial and error involved here, but in the end the box weights are as follows: A = 5 lbs.; B = 10 lbs.; C = 20 lbs. The weights are thus to be distributed as shown.

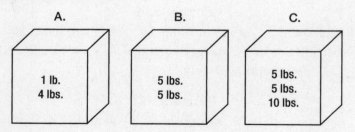

Chapter 4

Puzzle 1: 1
Dividing any number by 1, you get that number: $5 \div 1 = 5$; $89 \div 1 = 89$; $568 \div 1 = 568$; and so on.

Puzzle 2: 15
The number 15 is less than 20 and greater than 11, and it is the only number in this range (12, 13, 14, 15, 16, 17, 18, 19) that is divisible by five: $15 \div 5 = 3$.

Puzzle 3: 11
If you multiply 11 by 2, you will get 22; if you then add 2 to that result, you get 24: $11 \times 2 = 22 + 2 = 24$. No other number less than 20 will work out.

Puzzle 4: 3
Multiplying 3 by 11 you get 33; then subtracting 3 from this you get 30: $3 \times 11 = 33 - 3 = 30$.

Puzzle 5: 2
If you add 2 three times to 10, you will get 16; then if you divide 16 by 8, you get 2 back: $10 + 2 + 2 + 2 = 16 \div 8 = 2$. No other number will work out.

Puzzle 6: 4
Multiplying 4 by itself four times altogether produces 256. If you divide this by 64, you get 4 again: $4 \times 4 \times 4 \times 4 = 256 \div 64 = 4$. No other number will work.

Puzzle 7: 13
The prime number that works is 13. If you add 17 to 13, since 17 is the next highest prime number after 13, you get 30. Dividing 30 by 5 produces 6: $13 + 17 = 30 \div 5 = 6$. No other number will work.

Puzzle 8: 59

The prime number that works is 59. If you subtract 8 from 59, you will get 51; if you divide 51 by 17, you will get 3, which is a prime number: $59 - 8 = 51 \div 17 = 3$. Remember that the required number must be a prime number between 37 and 67, otherwise other possibilities will work!

Puzzle 9: 7

If you multiply 7 (a prime number less than 23 and greater than 5) by itself (7×7), you will get 49. If you then subtract 2 from this, you will get 47, a prime number itself: $7 \times 7 = 49 - 2 = 47$. Remember that the result must be a prime number between 40 and 50, otherwise other possibilities will work!

Puzzle 10: 36

If you divide 36 by 3, you get 12, which is divisible by 6: $36 \div 3 = 12 \div 6 = 2$. No other number will work.

Puzzle 11

5	5	2
5	4	6
1	2	3

Puzzle 13

2	9	9
8	8	4
10	3	7

Puzzle 12

8	2	3
1	2	10
4	9	0

Puzzle 14

7	3	3	3
5	5	0	6
8	0	8	0
5	5	5	1

Puzzle 15

4	4	3	3
4	4	6	3
8	8	1	3
2	2	8	9

Puzzle 18

2	3	3	8
4	1	2	7
5	1	3	9
1	1	1	3

Puzzle 16

7	3	3	7
8	2	9	1
4	7	1	8
1	8	7	4

Puzzle 19

5	1	1	5
1	0	0	1
1	0	0	1
5	1	1	5

Puzzle 17

5	7	9	2
8	2	9	4
7	9	1	6
3	5	4	11

Puzzle 20

1	3	3	1
2	5	5	2
2	5	5	2
1	3	3	1

Puzzle 21: 1, 2, 3, 6, 13

Puzzle 22: 4

Subtracting the two numbers in the middle produces the number at the top of the circle. Another explanation is that the number to the left in each circle is the sum of the other two numbers.

Puzzle 23: 8899

Adding the digits: $8 + 8 + 9 + 9 = 34$

2	3	5	2	7	7	5	4
1	8	8	9	9	0	2	3
6	3	3	0	5	6	6	9
8	6	2	1	4	9	5	1
8	7	8	8	9	9	9	2
3	4	5	3	4	9	5	6
1	2	4	5	6	3	2	1
8	9	0	5	4	1	9	2

Puzzle 24

As you can see, the solution path is made up of the number sequence: $1 + 2 + 0 + 3 + 4 + 0 + 1 + 2 + 2 + 2 + 1 + 1 + 1 + 3 = 23$.

7	1	1	3	2	4
7	2	0	1	0	5
7	8	3	9	8	5
4	4	4	0	8	7
7	8	9	1	2	8
0	9	8	2	2	3
6	5	7	8	2	9
4	5	7	8	1	9
1	0	3	6	1	5
5	5	5	5	1	5
5	9	8	6	3	5

Puzzle 25: 33

Twice 18 is 36, and three less than this is 33. Add the two together, $18 + 33$, and you get 51.

Chapter 5

Puzzle 1: A

The square stands for 1.
The pentagon stands for 5.
The triangle stands for 3.
$1 + 5 + 3 = 9$
$1 + 1 + 1 + 1 = 4$
$5 - 3 = 2$
$5 + 5$ (missing) $- 3 = 7$

Puzzle 2: B

The pentagon stands for 4.
The triangle stands for 5.
The circle stands for 3.
$4 \times 5 - 3 = 17$
$3 \times 3 = 9$
$4 \times 4 = 16$
$4 + 3 + 3$ (missing) $= 10$

Puzzle 3: C

The square stands for 7.
The triangle stands for 3.
The circle stands for 1.
$7 + 7 + 1 + 1 = 16$
$7 + 7 + 1 = 15$
$3 + 1 + 1 + 1 = 6$
$7 + 1 + 3 + 7$ (missing) $= 18$

Puzzle 4: D

The circle stands for 2.
The triangle stands for 3.
The square stands for 1.
The hexagon stands for 5.
$2 + 3 + 1 + 5 = 11$
$1 \times 5 \times 1 = 5$
$3 + 3 + 3 = 9$
$2 + 1 + 1 + 5$ (missing) $= 9$

Puzzle 5: D

The cube stands for 3.
The cylinder stands for 2.
The parallelogram stands for 1.
The diamond stands for 5.
$3 \times 2 = 6$
$1 + 2 = 3$
$1 \times 2 = 2$
$3 \times 5 = 15$
$3 + 2 + 5 = 10$ (missing number)

Puzzle 6: A

The pentagon stands for 4.
The square stands for 2.
The cube stands for 3.
The circle stands for 1.
$4 \times 2 = 8$
$3 \times 1 = 3$
$4 \times 3 = 12$
$2 \times 1 = 2$
$4 + 2 + 3 + 1 = 10$ (missing)

Puzzle 7: C

The cube stands for 5.
The square stands for 3.
The circle stands for 2.
The pentagon stands for 1.
$5 \times 3 = 15$
$3 + 2 = 5$
$2 \times 5 = 10$
$3 - 1 = 2$
$5 + 3 + 1 + 2 = 11$ (missing)

Puzzle 8: B

The circle stands for 2.
The square stands for 4.
The pentagon stands for 6.
The cube stands for 8.
$2 + 2 = 4$
$2 + 4 = 6$
$2 + 6 = 8$
$2 + 2 + 4 = 8$
$8 - 6 = 2$ (missing)

Puzzle 9: A

The circle stands for 10.
The square stands for 1.
The pentagon stands for 2.
The cube stands for 9.
$10 - 9 = 1$
$1 + 1 = 2$
$9 \times 1 = 9$
$9 + 1 = 10$
$1 \times 10 = 10$ (missing)

Puzzle 10: B

The cube stands for 7.
The pentagon stands for 5.
The cylinder stands for 12.
The diamond stands for 2.

$7 + 5 = 12$
$7 - 5 = 2$
$5 + 2 = 7$
$12 - 7 = 5$
$5 + 5 + 2 = 12$ (missing)

Puzzle 11: C

Did you miss this one? The missing figure is the triangle. The sequence is the reverse one to the illustration puzzle—that is, the number of sides diminishes by one, starting with the heptagon: heptagon (seven sides)—hexagon (six sides)—pentagon (five sides)—square (four sides)—missing triangle (three sides).

Puzzle 12: D

The number of internal lines in the squares increases by one sequentially.

Square 1 = one internal line
Square 2 = two internal lines
Square 3 = three internal lines
Square 4 = four internal lines

Next square in sequence = five internal lines = option D

Puzzle 13: A

This one is based on the reverse logic of the previous puzzle. The number of internal lines in the circles decreases by one sequentially.

Circle 1 = five internal lines
Circle 2 = four internal lines
Circle 3 = three internal lines
Circle 4 = two internal lines

Next circle in sequence = one internal line = option A

Puzzle 14: D

The number above a figure indicates the number of its sides. So the diamond figure has four sides.

Puzzle 15: C

The number above a figure stands for twice the number of its sides. The hexagon figure has six sides, and twice this is twelve.

Puzzle 16: A

The number above a figure stands for five times the number of its sides. The hexagon has six sides, and $6 \times 5 = 30$.

Puzzle 17: D

The number over a figure is one less than the number of its sides. The triangle has three sides, and one less than this is two.

Puzzle 18: C

The number over the two figures represents the sum of the number of their sides. A triangle has three sides and a pentagon has five. The sum is eight.

Puzzle 19: A

This time the number over the two figures represents the difference between the number of their sides. A hexagon has six sides and a triangle has three sides. The difference is three.

Puzzle 20: D

This is a tough one. Add the number of sides in the two figures and then subtract one from the sum. A heptagon has seven sides and a hexagon has six sides. Together they have thirteen sides. Subtract one from this and you get twelve.

Puzzle 21

Puzzle 22

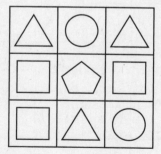

Puzzle 23

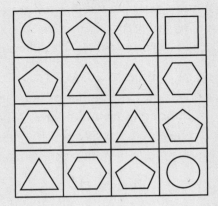

Puzzle 24

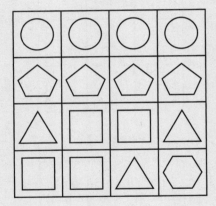

Puzzle 25

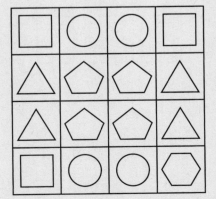

Chapter 6

Puzzle 1

```
    6  1  3
+   2  4  5
─────────────
    8  5  8
```

Puzzle 2

```
       4  1
    9  1  8
+   1  1  6
─────────────
 1  0  7  5
```

Puzzle 3

```
    6  0  9
    3  2  0  5
+   6  4  5  1
─────────────────
 1  0  2  6  5
```

Puzzle 4

```
    4  8  7
-   1  9  6
─────────────
    2  9  1
```

Puzzle 5

```
    8  8  0  0
-   5  5  7  8
─────────────────
    3  2  2  2
```

Puzzle 6

```
      1  2  0
   ×     8  1
   ─────────────
      1  2  0
   9  6  0
   ─────────────
   9  7  2  0
```

Puzzle 7

```
      5  2  5
   ×     4  5
   ─────────────
      2  6  2  5
   2  1  0  0
   ─────────────
   2  3  6  2  5
```

Puzzle 8

```
            1  0  2
   2  3 │ 2  3  4  6
          2  3
          ─────────
                4  6
                4  6
                ─────
                   0
```

Puzzle 9

```
            4  5  5
   1  2 │ 5  4  6  0
          4  8
          ─────────
             6  6
             6  0
          ─────────
                6  0
                6  0
                ─────
                   0
```

Puzzle 10

```
        5   9   5
    2   0   5   6
    6   4   5   1   3
+   1   0   2   6   5   5
─────────────────────
1   6   9   8   1   9
```

Puzzle 11

```
    6   5
+   3   5
─────────
1   0   0
```

Puzzle 12

```
    3   2   1
+   2   3   1
─────────────
    5   5   2
```

Puzzle 13

```
    3   0   0
+   9   5   5
─────────────
1   2   5   5
```

Puzzle 14

```
    5   0   1
−       9   0
─────────────
    4   1   1
```

Puzzle 15

```
  4  0  2  0
-    5  5  4
----------
  3  4  6  6
```

Puzzle 16

```
  5  4  0  1
-  1  4  0  5
----------
  3  9  9  6
```

Puzzle 17

```
  1  2  2  1
-     3  2  1
----------
     9  0  0
```

Puzzle 18

```
  1  2  3  1
  3  1  1  0
+ 3  0  4  0
----------
  7  3  8  1
```

Puzzle 19

```
  7  1  1  0
-     7  0  9
----------
  6  4  0  1
```

Puzzle 20

```
    5  0  7  2  0
    1  2  0  0  2
 +  1  5  2  5  5
   ──────────────
    7  7  9  7  7
```

Puzzle 21

$4 + 5 + 6 = 5 \times 3$

Puzzle 22

$2 (23 - 3) - 40 = 0$

Puzzle 23

$(5 \times 6) \div 10 = 7 - 4$

Puzzle 24

$2 + 2 + 2 + 2 + 2 = 9 + (4 - 3)$

Puzzle 25

$(99 \div 3) + 7 = 4 \times 10$

Chapter 7

Puzzle 1: Seven

The number of trips is exactly the same as those required by the original (illustration) puzzle.

The traveler takes his first trip across the river to the other bank taking the goat and leaving the two wolves safely behind.

He drops off the goat on the other bank and for his second trip goes back to the original side alone.

When he gets there, he picks up one of the two wolves and with that wolf takes his third trip across, leaving the other wolf alone on the original side.

When he gets to the other bank, he drops off the wolf and leaves it there. He picks up the goat; otherwise, the wolf would eat the goat. So for his fourth trip the traveler takes the goat as a passenger back to the original side.

When he gets there, he drops off the goat, picks up the other wolf, and takes his fifth trip across.

When he gets to the other bank, he drops off the wolf, leaving it together with the wolf that is already there, and takes a trip across back to the original side alone. This is his sixth trip.

When he gets to the original side, he picks up the goat and together takes the final trip across (the seventh trip). Of course, when he gets to the other bank this time, he has his two wolves and goat with him and can continue safely with his journey.

Puzzle 2: Seven

The traveler takes her first trip across the river to the other bank taking the wolf and leaving the two goats safely behind.

When she gets to the other bank, she drops off the wolf and goes back to the original side alone (second trip).

When she gets back, she picks up one of the two goats and goes across, leaving the other goat alone on the original side (third trip).

She drops off the goat on the other bank and picks up the wolf, otherwise, the wolf would eat the goat. So for her fourth trip the traveler takes the wolf as a passenger back to the original side.

When she gets there, she drops off the wolf, picks up the other goat, and takes the trip across to the other bank (fifth trip).

When she gets there, she drops off the goat, leaving it together with the other goat, and then makes the trip across back to the original side alone (sixth trip).

When she gets to the original side, she picks up the wolf and takes the final trip across (seventh trip). When she gets to the other bank, she has her wolf and two goats with her and can continue safely with her journey.

Puzzle 3: Seven

The traveler takes her first trip across the river to the other bank taking the goat and leaving the two cabbages safely behind.

She drops off the goat on the other bank and goes back to the original side alone (second trip).

When she gets there, she picks up one of the two cabbages and goes across to the other bank, leaving the other cabbage alone on the original side (third trip).

She drops off the cabbage on the other bank and picks up the goat to go back with her, otherwise the goat would eat that cabbage. So she goes back with the goat as a passenger (fourth trip).

When she arrives, she drops off the goat, picks up the cabbage, and goes across to the other bank (fifth trip).

When she gets there, she drops off the cabbage, leaving it together with the other cabbage, and takes a trip across back to the original side alone (sixth trip).

When she gets to the original side, she picks up the goat and together they take the final trip across (seventh trip). Of course, when she gets to the other bank this time, she has her goat and two cabbages with her and can continue safely with her journey.

Puzzle 4: Seven

The traveler takes his first trip across with the goat, leaving the wolf and two cabbages safely alone.

Once he gets there, he drops off the goat and goes back alone (second trip).

When he gets to the original side, he picks up the two cabbages and goes across to the other side (third trip). Remember that the boat can hold the traveler and the two cabbages.

Once he gets there, he drops off the two cabbages and goes back with the goat so that the goat will not eat the cabbages (fourth trip).

When he gets to the original side, he drops off the goat and goes back to the other bank with the wolf (fifth trip).

Once there, he drops off the wolf, leaving it with the two cabbages, and goes back alone (sixth trip).

When he gets to the original side, he picks up the goat and goes to the other bank (seventh trip). Once there, he can proceed with all intact.

Puzzle 5: Seven

Again, there are several ways to take the seven trips. Is there a hidden pattern here?

The traveler takes her first trip across the river to the other bank taking both goats with her, leaving the two cabbages safely alone on the original side with the wolf. She could have started with the goat and one cabbage. No matter—the end result would be the same.

When she is on the other bank, she drops off both goats and goes back to the original side alone (second trip).

On that side, she picks up the two cabbages and goes to the other side with them, leaving the wolf behind (third trip). She could have picked up the wolf and a cabbage, leaving the other cabbage behind. No matter—the end result would be the same.

Once on the other side, she drops off the two cabbages and goes back with the two goats, to avoid disaster (fourth trip).

When she arrives on the original side, she drops off the two goats, picks up the wolf, and goes over to the other bank (fifth trip).

Once there, she drops off the wolf, leaving it with the two cabbages, and makes her way back alone (sixth trip).

When she gets to the original side, she picks up the two goats and makes the trip over (seventh trip).

When she arrives, she has the wolf, the two goats, and the two heads of cabbage, intact, and thus can continue with her journey.

Puzzle 6: Seven (again!)

The traveler takes her first trip across the river to the other bank taking both goats with her, leaving the two cabbages safely alone on the original side with the two wolves.

When she is on the other bank, she drops off both goats and goes back to the original side alone (second trip).

On that side, she picks up the two wolves, leaving the two cabbages behind, and goes across to the other bank (third trip). She could have picked up a wolf and one cabbage—again, no difference in outcome.

On the other bank she drops off the wolves but goes back with the two goats, otherwise the wolves would eat them (fourth trip).

Once back on the original side, she drops off the two goats, picks up the two cabbages, and goes to the other bank (fifth trip).

Once there, she drops off the cabbages, leaving them harmlessly with the wolves. She then goes back to the original side alone (sixth trip).

When she gets there, she picks up the two goats and goes over to the other side (seventh trip). When she gets there, she has the two wolves, the two goats, and the two heads of cabbage, intact, and thus can continue with her journey.

Puzzle 7: Three

This is easier than it appears. The important trip is the first one. The traveler takes his first trip across the river to the other bank taking the ogre and the goat with him, leaving the wolf and cabbage safely alone on the original side. He could have started with the wolf and the goat. No matter—the result would have been the same.

When he is on the other bank, he drops off both the ogre and the goat, since the ogre does not eat goats, and he goes back to the original side alone (second trip).

Once there, he picks up the wolf and goat and goes to the other bank (third trip). When he gets there he will have the ogre, wolf, goat, and cabbage, intact, and thus can continue with his journey.

Puzzle 8: Five

The traveler starts by taking across the wolf and the cabbage, leaving the ogre, goat, and snake safely behind (first trip). She could have started with the wolf and the goat. No matter—the end result would have been the same.

Once she gets to the other bank, she drops off the wolf and cabbage safely and goes back alone (second trip).

When she gets to the original side, she picks up the snake and goes across to the other bank (third trip). There are alternatives here, but they all lead to the solution of five trips. You can try them out by yourself.

Once she gets to the other side, she drops off the snake, leaving it safely with the wolf and cabbage, and goes back alone (fourth trip).

When she gets to the original side she picks up the ogre and the goat and goes over to the other bank (fifth trip). Once there all is intact and she can continue with her journey.

Puzzle 9: Seven

The traveler takes his first trip across with the ogre and the goat (since the boat will hold the goat and one other along with the traveler). This allows him to leave the wolf, cabbage, and snake safely alone. The traveler could have started with the wolf and goat. No matter—the result is the same. You can try this alternative by yourself.

When he gets to the other bank, he drops the ogre and goat safely off and goes back alone (second trip).

Once he is back on the original side, he has various choices (and they might all work out as you can try for yourself). So, let's go with the snake. Remember that he can only take one without the goat. He goes across with the snake for his third trip.

When he gets there, he drops the snake off, leaving it safely with the ogre and goat. He goes back alone (fourth trip). He could have gone back with the goat, but this does not change the number of trips required.

Once he gets back to the original side, he picks up the cabbage and goes back to the other bank (fifth trip).

Once he gets there he drops the cabbage off but picks up the goat, for obvious reasons, and goes back with the goat (sixth trip).

When he gets back to the original side, he picks up the wolf and with the goat already on board goes to the other bank (seventh trip). When he gets there, he is ready to go on with his journey.

Again, note that there are other ways to plan the trips back and forth, but they all will yield the same result—seven.

Puzzle 10: Nine

The traveler picks up the goat, leaving the wolf, cabbage, and snake safely alone. She goes over to the other side with the goat (first trip).

On the other side she drops off the goat and goes back alone (second trip).

When she gets to the original side, she has several options, but let's go with the snake. Others will work as you can find out by yourself. So, she goes over with the snake, leaving the wolf and cabbage safely behind (third trip).

When she gets to the other bank, she drops off the snake, leaving it safely with the goat and goes back alone (fourth trip).

When she arrives on the original side, she can pick up the wolf or cabbage. Either one will work. Let's go with the wolf. So, for her fifth trip (over to the other bank) she carries the wolf.

On the other bank she drops off the wolf, but takes the goat back with her (for obvious reasons). This is her sixth trip.

When she gets back to the original side, she drops off the goat and goes back with the cabbage (seventh trip).

When she gets to the other side, she drops off the cabbage, leaving it with the wolf and snake, and goes back for the goat alone (eighth trip).

When she gets to the original side, she picks up the goat, goes over, and with the others continues on her journey (ninth trip).

Puzzle 11: Five

The two men go across together leaving the woman alone (first trip).

When they get to the other side, one of the men steps off and the other one goes back alone (second trip).

Once he gets back to the original side, he steps off and the woman gets on and goes to the other side alone (third trip).

Once she gets to the other bank, she steps off, and the man there gets on and goes back to the original side alone (fourth trip).

When he gets there, he picks up the other man and they go together over to the other side (fifth trip). Once there, they reunite with the woman and are on their way.

Puzzle 12: Five

The logic is exactly the same as for the previous puzzle.

The two women start by going over together, leaving the man alone (first trip).

Once they get to the other side, one gets off and the other goes back alone (second trip).

When she gets to the original side, she gets off, and the man gets on, going over to the other side alone (third trip).

Once he gets there, he steps off and the woman there gets on and goes back alone (fourth trip).

When she arrives, she picks up the other woman and together they go over to the other side (fifth trip). There they reunite with the man and continue with their journey.

Puzzle 13: Five

Either the two men or the two women together could take the first trip. Either option will work. Let's go with the two men.

When they get to the other side, one steps off and the other goes back alone (second trip).

Once there, he steps off and the two women go over together (third trip).

When they get to the other side, they step off and the man who was there gets on and goes back alone (fourth trip).

Once he gets to the original side, he picks up the other man and they go over together (fifth trip). There they reunite with the women and continue with their journey.

Puzzle 14: Three

There are a few ways to plan the trips back and forth, but the end result should be the same—three trips in total. Here's one plan of attack:

The woman and the cat take the first trip over to the other bank, leaving the man alone on the original side. We could have started with the man and woman going over, leaving the cat alone, but the end result would be the same.

When they get there, the cat is dropped off and the woman goes back alone (second trip across).

When she gets back to the original side, she picks up the man and together they go over to the other bank where the cat is waiting for them (third trip), ready to continue on with their journey.

Puzzle 15: Seven

There are several ways to plan the trips back and forth, but the end result will be the same—seven trips in total. Here's one solution:

One woman and the cat take the first trip over to the other bank, leaving the two men and the other woman alone on the original side.

When they get there, the cat is dropped off and the woman goes back alone (second trip).

When she gets back to the original side, she picks up the other woman and together they go over to the other bank where the cat is waiting for them (third trip).

One of the two women gets off to stay with the cat and the other goes back alone (fourth trip).

When she gets back, she picks up one of the men and goes with him across to the other side, leaving the other man alone (fifth trip). Note: the woman could have gotten off herself and let the two men go across. Either way, the number of trips needed is not altered in any way.

When the man and the woman get to the other bank, she gets off and the man goes back alone (sixth trip). The other option is for the man to get off and the woman to go back. No matter—this would not change the end result.

When he gets back to the original side, he picks up the other man and the two go across to the other bank where the two women and the cat are waiting for them to continue on with their journey (seventh trip).

Puzzle 16: Seven

For the first trip the man and woman go over together to the other side.

Once there, the man steps off and the woman goes back alone (second trip).

When she gets to the original side, she can pick up either animal. Let's go with the cat. You can try it with the dog if you wish—the result will be the same. So, she goes over with the cat for the third trip.

Once she gets to the other side, she drops off the cat and goes back with the man, in order not to leave him alone with the cat (fourth trip).

When they get to the original side, the man steps off and the woman goes to the other side with the dog (fifth trip).

Once she gets over to the other bank, she drops off the dog and goes back to the original side alone (sixth trip).

When she gets there, she picks up the man and together they go over to the other bank, where the animals are waiting for all to continue with the journey (seventh trip).

Puzzle 17: Five

For the first trip, the two men go over together to the other side, leaving the woman and the cat alone.

Once there, one of the men steps off and the other goes back alone (second trip).

Once he gets to the original side, he picks up the woman, leaving the cat, and together they go over to the other side (third trip).

When they get there, the man steps off to stay with the other man and the woman goes back alone (fourth trip).

When she gets back to the original side, she picks up the cat and together they go over to the other bank to meet up with the two men and continue with their journey (fifth trip).

Puzzle 18: Seven

There are different ways to plan the trips back and forth, but the end result should be the same—seven trips in total. Here's one plan:

The man goes over with one dog (allowed) to the other side (first trip). An alternative would be to start with the woman and the cat (allowed); but as mentioned the end result will be the same.

When the man and dog reach the other side, the dog is dropped off and the man goes back alone (second trip).

When he gets back to the original side, he can pick up the woman or the other dog (but not the cat, as we are told). Let's go with the dog. Either way it will work out. So, he goes over with that dog to the other side (third trip).

Once there he drops off the second dog, so that there are now two dogs on the other side. He goes back alone (fourth trip).

When he arrives on the original side, he steps off and the woman and cat get on and go over to the other side—this is the only permissible arrangement with the cat on the boat (fifth trip).

Once she gets there, she drops off the cat, leaving it with the two dogs. She then goes back to the original side alone (sixth trip).

When she gets there she picks up the man and together they go across to the other side, where the animals are waiting for them so that they can all continue with the journey (seventh trip).

Puzzle 19: Five

The brother starts by taking one of the dogs over (permitted) (first trip).

When he gets to the other side, he drops off the dog and goes back alone (second trip).

Once he gets to the original side, he picks up the sister, leaving the other dog alone and the two go over on the boat (permitted) (third trip).

When they get to the other side, the sister steps off and joins the first dog. The brother goes back alone (fourth trip).

Once he gets back to the original side, he picks up the other dog and together they go over to the other side to join the other two and continue with the journey (fifth trip).

Puzzle 20: Nine

The two brothers take the first trip over, leaving the two sisters with the two dogs (permitted). We could have started with a brother and a sister. No matter—the end result would be the same.

Once they get to the other side, one of the brothers steps off and the other one goes back alone (second trip).

When he arrives on the original side, he picks up one of the sisters, leaving the other with the two dogs (required). Together they go over to the other side (third trip).

Once they get there, the sister steps off to join the brother already there and the brother on the boat goes back alone (fourth trip).

When he gets back to the original side, he picks up one of the two dogs, leaving a sister with the other dog behind (required). They go over to the other side (fifth trip).

Once there, the dog is dropped off to stay with the sister and brother there (permitted). The brother on the boat goes back alone to the original side (sixth trip).

Once he gets there he picks up the dog, leaving the sister behind. They go over together (seventh trip).

Once there he drops off the dog. There are now two dogs, a brother, and a sister on the other side. The brother on the boat goes back to the original side alone (eighth trip).

When he gets to the original side, he picks up the second sister and together they go over to the other side to join the others and continue their journey (ninth trip).

Puzzle 21: Five

Since the cat must go over first, and the brother last, it is the sister who must go over with the cat for the first trip.

When they get to the other side, the cat is dropped off and the sister goes back alone (second trip).

Once she gets to the original side, she picks up the dog, leaving the brother there for last. Together they go to the other side (third trip).

When they get there, the dog is dropped off to stay with the cat and the sister goes back alone (fourth trip).

Once she gets to the other side, she picks up the brother and together they go over to meet up with the cat and dog and continue on their way (fifth trip).

Puzzle 22: Five

The first trip is taken by the sister and mother over to the other side. This ensures that it is the sister who takes the second trip alone.

Once they are on the other side, the mother gets off and the sister goes back alone, as required (second trip).

When she gets to the original side, she steps off in view of the brother taking the fourth trip alone. The brother and father get on and go over to the other side (third trip).

Once there the father gets off to stay with the mother and the brother goes back alone, as required (fourth trip).

When he gets there, he picks up the sister and together they go over to the other side to join their parents and continue on their journey (fifth trip).

Puzzle 23: Seven

The traveler starts by taking the two wolves over, leaving the three goats harmlessly behind (first trip).

Once on the other side, the two wolves are dropped off and the traveler goes back alone (second trip).

When she gets to the original side, she picks up two of the three goats, leaving one behind, and goes over to the other side (third trip).

Once there, she drops off the two goats and picks up the two wolves, needless to say. Together they go back (fourth trip).

When they get to the original side, the two wolves are dropped off and the remaining goat is picked up to go over to the other side (fifth trip).

Once there, the goat is dropped off to stay with the other two goats already there. The traveler goes back alone (sixth trip).

When she gets to the original side, she picks up the two wolves there and together they go over to the other side to join the goats and go on their way (seventh trip).

Puzzle 24: Seven

The traveler starts by taking over the two wolves, leaving the two ogres and two goats safely behind (first trip).

Once on the other side, she leaves the two wolves and goes back alone (second trip).

When she gets to the original side, she can pick up either pair. Either one will work. Let's go with the two ogres. She goes over with them to the other side, leaving the two goats behind (third trip).

Once there, she drops off the ogres but picks up the wolves and goes back with them to avoid disaster (fourth trip).

When she gets back to the original side, she drops off the wolves and goes back to the other side with the two goats (fifth trip).

Once there, she drops off the two goats safely with the two ogres and goes back alone (sixth trip).

When she gets back to the original side, she picks up the two wolves and goes over to meet up with the other animals and continue the journey (seventh trip).

Puzzle 25: Impossible

There is no way to make the trips back and forth safely in this way, as you might want to confirm by yourself.

Chapter 8

Puzzle 1

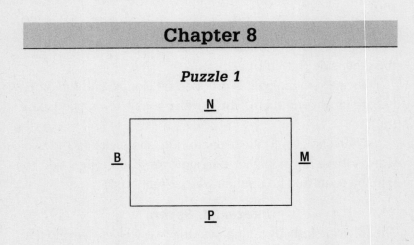

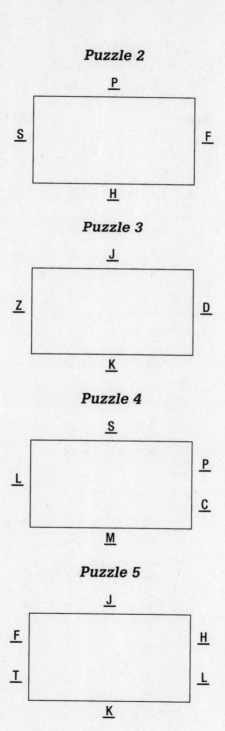

Puzzle 2

P

S   F

H

Puzzle 3

J

Z   D

K

Puzzle 4

S

L   P

C

M

Puzzle 5

J

F   H

T   L

K

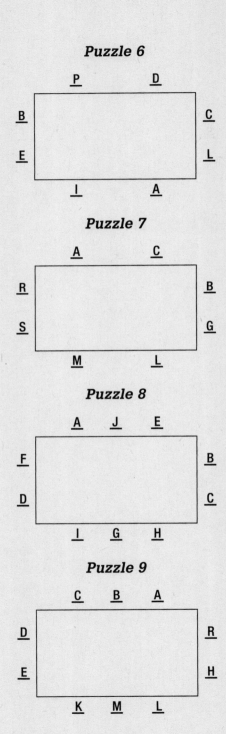

Puzzle 6

P   D

B   C

E   L

I   A

Puzzle 7

A   C

R   B

S   G

M   L

Puzzle 8

A   J   E

F   B

D   C

I   G   H

Puzzle 9

C   B   A

D   R

E   H

K   M   L

Puzzle 10

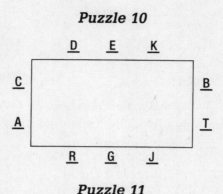

Puzzle 11

Andy—Emma
Bill—Dina
Chuck—Nina

Andy refuses to pair off with Dina, and she refuses to pair off with Chuck. The only possibility left for Dina is with Bill. Chuck refuses to pair off with Emma. He also cannot be paired off with Dina (since she's Bill's partner). So only Nina is left for him. This leaves Andy and Emma as the third couple.

Puzzle 12

Andrea—Rita
Bea—Mary
Lara—Noreen

Andrea, Bea, Rita, and Mary refuse to play with Noreen. So the only partner left for Noreen is Lara. Bea and Rita refuse to play with each other. And Bea refuses to play with Andrea. This leaves Mary as the only possibility for Bea. The last pairing is Andrea and Rita.

Puzzle 13

Alex—Lucky
Billy—Manny
Nicky—Ron

Alex is paired with Lucky. Manny refuses to play with Nicky or Ron. So the only possibility for Manny is with Billy. This leaves Nicky and Ron as the third pair.

Puzzle 14: Pat

From (1) and (2), we know that Helen does not want to go out with Gus or any of his friends—Art and Charles. So this leaves the other two—Jack and Pat. From (3), we know that she has gone out with Jack and desires to go out with someone else, namely Pat. That's what she does.

Puzzle 15: Charlotte

From (1), we exclude Pina as a partner for Trina. From (2), we exclude Guy and Amy. From (3), we exclude Jasmine. So this leaves Charlotte.

Puzzle 16

Alex—Claudia
Mark—Paula
Len—Delia

If Claudia is not paired with Mark or Len, the only possibility for her is Alex, since each pair must have a boy and a girl. If Mark is not paired with Delia, and of course not with Claudia either (Alex is), this leaves Paula as the only possible partner for him. The remaining pair consists of Len and Delia.

Puzzle 17

Andrew—Becky
Crandall—Dora
Ella—Greta
Ivan—Pavi

From (2), (3), and (4), we know that Andrew has already played with Dora, Greta, Pavi, Ivan, Ella, and Crandall. This leaves Becky as the only possibility for him.

Ivan has played against Ella and Crandall (3), as well as against Dora and Greta (5). We know that Andrew and Becky are paired. So this leaves Pavi for Ivan.

Greta has played against Crandall and Dora (6). And since we already have two pairings, Andrew with Becky and Ivan with Pavi, this leaves Ella as the only possible partner for Greta.

Crandall and Dora are the remaining pair.

Puzzle 18

Art—Mark
Bill—Greg
Lucia—Yolanda
Ken—Zina

From (1) and (2), we can eliminate the following pairings for Lucia: Lucia—Bill, Lucia—Greg, Lucia—Art, Lucia—Ken, and Lucia—Zina. We also know that the pairing Lucia with Mark is wrong, since it is on the original scorecard. So this leaves Yolanda as the only possible partner for Lucia.

From (3) we can eliminate the following pairings: Art—Bill, Art—Greg, and Art—Ken, and we know that Art—Zina is a mistake (from the original scorecard). We already know that Lucia and Yolanda are a pair. So we can eliminate them as well as possible partners for Art. This leaves Art and Mark as a pair.

From (4), we can eliminate Bill—Ken and Bill—Zina. Since we have already paired off Art, Mark, Lucia, and Yolanda. This leaves Greg as the only possible partner for Bill.

The final pair is Ken and Zina.

Puzzle 19

Andy—Irma
Barney—Jill
Charlie—Dave
Ed—Fiona
Hillary—Gaia

Every once in a while we will insert an easy puzzle in the difficult section, just to keep you on your toes. This is such a puzzle.

From (2), we can establish the following two pairings: Charlie—Dave and Ed—Fiona. From (3), we can also establish the pair of Hillary—Gaia. Now, from (1) we eliminate Irma as a partner for Barney. So which woman is left for Barney? It is Jill. This leaves Andy and Irma as the final pairing.

Puzzle 20

Andrew—Nora
Bob—Ella
Chuck—Debbie

From (1), we deduce that Andrew is the oldest of the three men, followed by Bob and then Chuck, who is the youngest. From (2), we can eliminate Ella or Nora as Chuck's partner, because they refuse to go out with anyone younger than Bob. So this leaves Debbie as the only possibility for Chuck.

From (3), we deduce that Debbie is the tallest followed by Ella and then Nora, who is the shortest. From (4), we can eliminate Nora as a pairing for Bob, because he refuses to go out with the shortest woman. We have already one pair, Chuck and Debbie, so this leaves Bob and Ella as a pair.

The last pair is, therefore, Andrew and Nora.

Puzzle 21

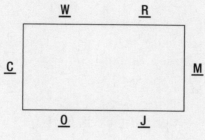

Puzzle 22

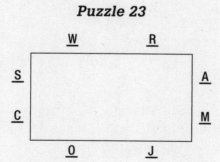

Puzzle 23

W   R

S   A

C   M

O   J

Puzzle 24

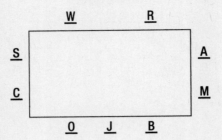

Puzzle 25

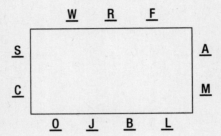